Buenos Aires

Buenos Aires

Nick Caistor

INNERCITIES
Signal Books

First published in 2014 by
Signal Books Limited
36 Minster Road
Oxford OX4 1LY
www.signalbooks.co.uk

A catalogue record for this book is available from the British Library

ISBN 978-1-904955-84-9 Paper

Cover Design: Imprint Digital Ltd.
Production: Imprint Digital Ltd.
Cover Images: Lee Torrens/Shutterstock; Cadaverexquisito/Wikimedia
Commons
Printed in India

Contents

Introduction

The first attempt to set up the colony of Nuestra Señora de los Buenos Ayres ended in dismal failure. By the time the second foundation took place, in 1580, it was obvious that despite the name Río de la Plata (River of Silver) next to which it was built, the settlement did not contain any precious metal. Nor had the estuary offered the desired short-cut to the Pacific Ocean and lucrative trade with Asia. Despite these dashed hopes, the distant outpost of the Spanish empire clung to the flank of the American continent on its bluff above one of the world's muddiest rivers. Rather than silver or gold, it was the cows and horses brought by the first settlers that were to determine the city's future and provide it with riches.

The streets of the new port were laid out like a chess-board according to Spanish imperial dictates, but Spain could do little to control the city's thriving contraband trade with other European countries. At the outset of the nineteenth century, when the war of independence from Spain began in earnest, Buenos Aires was still a *gran aldea*, a big village enclosed within its colonial boundaries and facing a hostile hinterland. Over the next hundred years, the city grew vertiginously. Hundreds of thousands of immigrants from all over Europe provided it with a unique mix of cultures, languages and customs. By the first decade of the twentieth century, the Argentine capital considered itself a close cousin of Paris, London or Berlin. The fine buildings on its newly built avenues, the vast new opera house, the bustling port—all these reflected the city's brash confidence in a bright future.

The decades that followed darkened this dream. Teeming slums grew up alongside belle époque palaces. The city's streets and squares frequently became battlegrounds, where the newcomers fought for a greater say in the country's political life and were resisted by the old order, backed by the armed forces. Buenos Aires bore the scars of these battles, while writers, musicians and painters sought other worlds that might offer compensation, at least in the imagination. In the 1930s Jorge Luis Borges and his friend, the mystical artist Xul Solar, turned the Argentine capital into a mysterious domain where anything could happen. The tango was danced and sung across the city from the insalubrious docks in La Boca to the smart salons of Avenida Alvear to soothe the nostalgia for other times and other places. The city grew into a metropolis that to the writer Ezequiel Martínez Estrada seemed like a giant's head on the puny body of the rest of Argentina.

Now, after four hundred years' existence, Buenos Aires still clings to the side of the continent, uncertain whether to embrace its Latin American identity or to reach out across the Atlantic to its imagined family. The city of today can still offer quiet suburban streets lined with blazing jacaranda trees; the noise and bustle of what the tango singer Carlos Gardel called *el músculo grande* (the great muscle) of the centre, flexing and straining; and a huge variety of communities each adding, in the words of his most famous song, a poignant flavour to their "beloved Buenos Aires".

A traditional *fileteado*, an elaborate painted street sign, featuring Carlos Gardel (Beatriz Vicente Britos/Wikimedia Commons)

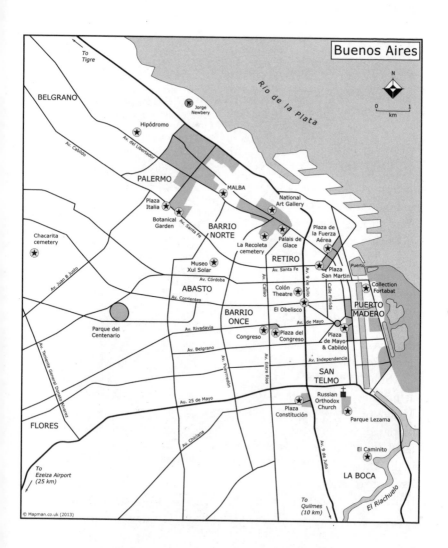

1

Topography
River and Plains

The River Riachuelo is one of the most polluted rivers in the world. For centuries, ocean-going ships have loaded and unloaded goods at the mouth of this sixty-kilometre long river: the waste from hides and the tanning industry, carcasses and salted meat, metallic ores, timber from the northern jungles of Argentina, wheat from the pampas, wine from the western province of Mendoza, as well as sewage from the giant city behind, have turned its waters into a heady stew of chemicals and dirt.

Yet almost five hundred years ago, the Riachuelo (Little River) looked very different. Situated close to one of the few low promontories on the southern shore of the vast estuary of the Río de la Plata (the "River of Silver" that is alluded to in the English translation, the River Plate) it provided welcome shelter and protection, as well as offering a source of fresh water for the first European explorers.

Situated at more than 34 degrees south, Buenos Aires is at roughly the same latitude as Cape Town in South Africa or Melbourne in Australia. Temperatures vary between the mid-30s centigrade in summer (January to April) and near freezing in winter (July and August), with only very rare falls of snow (last recorded in the winter of 2008). This Mediterranean climate has helped make its southern European settlers feel at home, especially as imported fruits like grapes, figs or peaches grow abundantly.

The First Settlement

In the early sixteenth century, captains such as Sebastian Cabot and Magellan began to make incursions into the two hundred-kilometre-wide Río de la Plata estuary. Like Columbus in the Caribbean before them, these navigators were searching for the passage round the southern tip of America that would open up a trade route between Europe and the Far East. Although the estuary is at a similar

The docks, c.1910 (Library of Congress, Washington DC)

latitude to the southernmost parts of Africa, the early European explorers were frustrated in their attempts to find a way through to the Pacific, and eventually had to sail several thousand more kilometres further south before they discovered the channels round Cape Horn. In 1516, one of these explorers, the Spaniard Juan Díaz de Solís, sailed into the wide river that he named the Mar Dulce or "Sweet Sea", which he hoped would lead directly to the Pacific Ocean. Unfortunately, soon after disembarking, he and most of his crew were killed by the indigenous Querandí Indians. A few survivors from this expedition heard tales of a fabulously rich country further inland, and it was these stories of gold and silver waiting to be discovered that led to the estuary (said to be the widest in the world, covering some 36,000 square kilometres) to be renamed the Río de la Plata.

However, it was not until February 1536 that the Spaniard Don Pedro de Mendoza brought his ships into the Riachuelo on the southern bank of the huge river. This time the intention was to found a lasting colony. Charles V of Spain had supplied Mendoza with more than a thousand men and thirteen ships for the venture, and appointed him governor of all the lands he might conquer in South America. In return, he was to build "three stone fortresses", and use the horses and cattle sent with him to establish a settlement that could help counteract the influence of Portugal on the Atlantic coast of Brazil. Sailing across the River Plate from an initial base in today's Uruguay, Pedro de Mendoza and his men created the small fort of Buenos Aires ("Good Winds") on top of the hill next to the Riachuelo.

As was common in those days, Mendoza's men were drawn from many parts of the Spanish empire, and it was a soldier from territories in Germany, Ulrich Schmidl, who provided the first description of the founding of Buenos Aires. Schmidl, whose statue stands in Parque Lezama close to where the original fort was built, recollected in old age what he had seen during his eighteen years in the Americas (the first edition of his *Derrotero y viaje a España y las Indias:* (Logbook of a Journey to Spain and the Indies), was published in Frankfurt in 1567). Unlike Bernal Díaz del Castillo, who spoke of the wonders of Mexico City and the riches of the Aztec civilization that Hernán Cortés had encountered and conquered some twenty years earlier, Schmidl describes the local Querandí Indians as leading a poor, nomadic life with no fixed communities. Unsure of the welcome these indigenous groups might give them, the Spaniards at once set about building a defensive fortress. According to Schmidl, they surrounded their encampment with "three-foot thick adobe walls the height a man with a sword can reach". Inside, the buildings apparently followed no pattern, although according to the probably fanciful engraving that accompanied the second printing of Schmidl's text, Don Pedro de Mendoza's house was a substantial three-storey building that would not have looked out of place in Madrid or Munich. There was also a rudimentary church, built out of the timbers of one of their ships.

Relations with the indigenous Querandíes quickly turned sour. In one battle Mendoza's son Diego, six horsemen and twenty foot-soldiers were killed, together with, as Schmidl laconically notes, 'more or less a thousand Indians'. This open hostility soon meant that the Spaniards were under almost constant siege in their fort, and as a result the would-be colonists faced a desperate shortage of food. Schmidl recounts one particularly gruesome episode: 'three Spaniards stole a horse and ate it in secret'. The men were found out, tortured and summarily hanged. But this was not the worst of it: 'when night fell, and everyone returned to their houses, some more Spaniards cut off the thighs and other parts of the hanged men, took them home, and ate them too.'

By this time, Don Pedro de Mendoza himself was dying of the "French disease", or syphilis. Seeing how desperate the situation was in the tiny fort of Buenos Aires, he sent his lieutenant Juan Ayolas with most of the men on an expedition upriver in order to discover whether there was anywhere with less hostile natives and land more suitable for agriculture. Ayolas sailed hundreds of kilometres up the River Paraná, and in 1537 his men founded Asunción de Paraguay. This new settlement was closer to the already established Spanish colonies in Peru to the north. It also offered more opportunities for obtaining and growing food, so that soon afterwards the few remaining colonists at Buenos Aires abandoned their fortress and moved to Asunción. They did, however, leave behind many of the horses and cattle brought by Don Pedro de Mendoza, which thrived on the rich grasslands around the settlement. A few centuries later, it was these animals, rather than any dreamt-of gold and silver, which were to form the basis of Argentina's riches.

It was not until 11 June 1580 that Buenos Aires (officially named la Ciudad de la Santísima Trinidad y Puerto de los Buenos Ayres) was founded for a second time, this time successfully. The leader of the Spaniards on this expedition was the Basque Juan de Garay, who sailed down the Río de la Plata from the thriving settlement in Paraguay with some sixty men and women.

Although the new colony was once again built round a fortress atop the hill (no more than thirty metres in height) next to the Riachuelo, Juan de Garay adopted the layout prescribed for Spanish cities in the New World established in the *Ordenanzas de Poblaciones* published by the Spanish King Felipe II in 1573. Following this template, the Plaza Mayor (later to become the Plaza de Mayo) was the hub from which the rest of the city developed. The natural boundaries of the city lay between the River Riachuelo-Matanza to the south, and the Rivers Luján and Reconquista, which drained into the estuary of the Paraná at the Tigre Delta some forty kilometres to the north-west.

As Buenos Aires was principally a port, the main square was placed behind the fortress on the bank above the river, rather than in a new centre. The square, covering one block from north to south, but two from east to west, contained the main garrison and the governor's palace, the cathedral and the seat of local government or *cabildo*. Stretching out from the square, the buildings followed a strict grid pattern, with blocks (*manzanas*) of approximately a hundred metres square. Beyond this grid of regular streets, de Garay also planned *chacras* or small farms. From the start therefore, given the lack of any truly defining geographical features, the limits of the city were established by administrative decision. Yet being so close to the water also meant that many parts of the capital have always been susceptible to flooding: the port area of La Boca next to the River Riachuelo is still frequently inundated. To counteract this threat, two deep ditches or *zanjones* were dug, one to the south of the city, the other to the north. As well as helping with drainage, they acted as a defence against the indigenous Indians, who still launched occasional attacks on the European settlers. These *zanjones* also became the boundaries for the growth of the city of Buenos Aires, until they were covered over in the nineteenth century as the population expanded rapidly.

This basic structure of the inner city remained the same throughout the seventeenth and eighteenth centuries. The main new buildings were the churches of El Pilar, Santo Domingo, Las Catalinas, San Francisco and San Ignacio, as well as more administrative offices for the Spanish crown. But Buenos Aires was a backwater; during the two centuries that Peru and its capital Lima formed the centre of the Spanish empire in South America, the cities closer to it such as Tucumán or Salta in Argentina's interior were more important as trading centres, while Buenos Aires remained little more than a village. Its population grew slowly from less than a thousand at the turn of the seventeenth century to only around 25,000 two hundred years later at the start of the nineteenth. Apart from the official buildings, the main architectural characteristic were the homes of the inhabitants: low, one-storey buildings made of adobe, with straw roofs, often with fig and lemon trees in their patios, and entirely lacking the grandeur of the imperial buildings of Peru or Mexico.

Nearly all of the port's trade was based on products from the nearby pampas. By the early nineteenth century, travellers were noting how the meat salting and tanning industries that had grown up on the south bank of the river Riachuelo had created a ghastly atmosphere. These *saladeros* were known as the "killing grounds": the area covering many hectares where the thousands of sheep and cattle driven in by the *gauchos* from the pampas were slaughtered.

The lack of any other defining features in the landscape seems to have made these *saladeros* even more noteworthy, especially as the few low huts situated there were often fenced off with high walls made up of the skulls of slaughtered animals. Because their meat could not be preserved for the long journey to European countries until refrigeration was developed late in the nineteenth century, the carcasses of all these butchered animals were simply thrown away to rot. The hides and fat (used for tallow candles) were removed, and the blood and offal left to coat the ground with a thick layer of foul-smelling detritus. This open-air slaughterhouse was close by the main road south out of the city, so that anyone leaving or entering Buenos Aires by that route had to cover their faces and ride as quickly as they could to escape the stench and the carrion. And of course, great quantities of this disgusting muck eventually found its way into the Riachuelo.

It was only after the fight for independence in the second decade of the nineteenth century that the face of Buenos Aires began to change dramatically. Over the next 150 years it became one of the most densely populated cities in the world, with new neighbourhoods quickly spreading out in all directions from the old city centre. This chaotic growth has meant there are few green spaces; there are no hills or rocky outcrops to vary the panorama, no lakes apart from the artificial ones at the park in the Palermo district, and all the small rivers draining into the Río de la Plata have been channelled underground. In fact, the streets are so level that no drivers park cars using a handbrake: one of the oddest sights newcomers to the city may see is that of a car sailing out into the middle of a street as it is pushed out of line by another impatient car owner—it is also the reason why it is never wise to try to cross a road by stepping between cars parked in a row. The view throughout the city is almost exclusively one of buildings and rectilinear streets: skyscrapers and tall apartment blocks in the centre, lower individual dwellings in the city's 47 boroughs. Apart from the grid system there has been little coherent town planning, so that every ten metres or so there can be a completely different style of building, leading to juxtapositions that can be startling, sometimes confusing, or simply an eyesore.

The Silver River

The inhabitants of Buenos Aires are known as *porteños*, people of the port. And yet almost from the foundation of the city, their relationship with the river has been ambivalent. There are no sandy beaches or spectacular riverine sights from either land or water. In its endless flow, the river can seem unwelcoming: one writer has even called it "unmoving", in its constant, unrelenting sweep. When the English naturalist Charles Darwin visited Buenos Aires, recorded in his famous *Voyage of the Beagle* (1839), he was distinctly unimpressed: "Our passage was a very long and tedious one. The Plata looks like a noble estuary on the map; but is in truth a poor affair. A wide expanse of muddy water that has neither grandeur nor beauty. At one time of the day, the two shores, both of which are extremely low, could just be distinguished from the deck."

The fact that from Buenos Aires itself the opposite bank (in Uruguay, which became the "Oriental Republic", or the republic on the eastern bank) is too far away to be visible robs the broad estuary of any feeling of connection with other people. For more than two centuries, while still under Spanish control, Buenos Aires was not legally permitted to send exports—in those days chiefly of tallow and hides—directly across the Atlantic back to Spain. Instead, all goods had to undertake the lengthy mule journey up through the Andes to the port of Callao in Peru, or further north still. Possibly this prohibition is at the root of the widespread sense that the city turns its back on the Río de la Plata, as if unwilling to acknowledge its existence.

At Buenos Aires, the Río de la Plata is still fresh water, but it is so broad that some geographers still prefer to classify it as an "inland sea". The water is usually a dull muddy brown in colour (although one poetic Argentine author preferred to call it the "colour of a tawny lion"). This is because the Paraná and Paraguay rivers which flow into it at the Tigre Delta some thirty kilometres north of the city bring ton upon ton of silt and sand down from the heart of the South American continent. The Tigre Delta itself is dotted with hundreds of small islands created by these alluvial deposits. Many of these have now been occupied by weekend and holiday homes for *porteños*, or offer sporting and barbecue facilities for trade union members and social clubs. (One of the best ways to take in the way that the Río de la Plata landscape changes dramatically from the grasslands to the already sub-tropical vegetation of the Tigre Delta is to take the famous cream-coloured No. 60 bus (*colectivo*) that goes all the way from Plaza in the centre of Buenos Aires to the Tigre Hotel.)

The currents of the Río de la Plata bring much of this silt to the Argentine side of the river, leaving Montevideo and the Uruguayan bank with much clearer water. On the Buenos Aires side, the river is often little more than a metre or two deep, and so to function as a port it has to be constantly dredged. These continual deposits have also meant that from the nineteenth century onwards, the physiognomy of the waterside has changed considerably. A watercolour from the 1790s shows the original fortress, the *cabildo* and the cathedral still perched directly above the riverbank. The Anglo-Argentine writer W. H. Hudson, born in 1841, describes his first visit to Buenos Aires at the age of six in *Far Away and Long Ago*. He speaks of the city centre being perched on a cliff, and remembers the view over "the front": "always with the vast expanse of water on one hand, with many big ships looking dim in the distance, and numerous lighters or berlanders coming from them with cargoes of merchandise which they unloaded into carts, these going about a quarter of a mile in the shallow water to meet them."

Due to the rapid expansion of trade with Europe in the second half of the nineteenth century, the Buenos Aires authorities decided to make it easier for these ships to come directly into port. A canal was dug to connect the River Riachuelo straight out to the Río de la Plata at what became known as the Vuelta de Rocha. As a result, what had previously been the mouth of the Riachuelo quickly silted up. In the 1830s the first two wooden quays were built, followed in the last years of the century by the construction of an artificial port at its old mouth. This port was made up of two enclosed docks with four piers projecting out into the river, almost directly beneath the original promontory. This area at the bottom of the cliff by the dockside is still commonly known as El Bajo—the Lower Side.

The land next to the new port soon filled up with warehouses, customs buildings and the imposing Hotel de Inmigrantes, where the thousands of new arrivals to Argentina were processed. Other buildings included the majestic Retiro railway station: it is from the square outside the station, as one looks past the monument to the Argentines killed in the 1982 Malvinas/Falklands conflict up to the tall green trees of Plaza San Martín above, that one still has the best impression of what the old riverbank promontory must have looked like. El Bajo is where the city is linked to the outside world, with streams of lorries bringing loads of produce, minerals, cattle and sheep down to the docks. Every so often the flow of traffic and pedestrians comes to a halt to allow a seemingly endless goods train to rumble past.

Until the mid-twentieth century, it was still possible to bathe in the Río de la Plata within the city boundaries. A proper walled promenade known as the *costanera* was built along the water's edge northwards from the port. This became a place for picnics and barbecues, with stalls or *chiringuitos* offering the ubiquitous steaks, or more humbly *choripan*, the Argentine version of the hot dog, with a spicy Italian-style sausage in a dry bread roll. Until the 1950s this was also the place for popular *balnearios* or swimming places, where city dwellers could bathe and cool off when summer temperatures hit the high 30s centigrade. There were also cafés and open air dance halls, most prominent among them being the German-style brewery and restaurant, Munich, designed in 1927 by the Hungarian refugee Andrés Kálnay, very much in the spirit of the vanished Austro-Hungarian Empire. The Munich, like nearly all the German-style restaurants in Buenos Aires, has now closed, and houses the gloomy offices of the city's museums authority. Nearby stands one of the capital's most endearing monuments: the marble fountain designed by one of Argentina's earliest female sculptors, Lola Mora (Dolores Mora de Hernández). Around the fountain, a riot of naked young men struggle to control rampant horses, while above them the water nymphs or Nereids (the title of the sculpture) cavort around Venus, the goddess of love. The fountain was originally meant to be placed near the presidential palace in the centre of the city, but such was the outcry from the *gente bien* (stuffy middle-class society) in the early twentieth century that it was promptly removed and stuck in this out-of-the-way corner, only visited by those in the know. Another somewhat melancholy reminder of better days in the past is the nearby long pier built for the Club de Pescadores, the fishermen's club that thrived until the river became so polluted that no-one wanted to fish there anymore.

By the 1970s, apart from the steak houses, the river was mostly shunned by the city. The most expensive tall buildings in the centre of the city had stunning views of the Río de la Plata from their top floors, but were separated from it by six-lane highways and wasteland. However, this situation, when the working docks and container port were moved further north. The economic boom during Carlos Menem's presidency (1989-99) led to a huge amount of renewed interest and investment: the old warehouses were converted into lofts, restaurants and fashion boutiques, while the architect Philippe Starck designed a new international hotel, the renowned Spanish engineer Santiago Calatrava created a new bridge linking the old docks, a vast new art museum was built and skyscraper apartment blocks quickly rose in what was known as Puerto Madero. This new development meant that the river skyline in the centre of the city changed completely, as its inhabitants thrust out towards the water once more.

In was also decided to discontinue dredging in this downtown area, so that more land has been reclaimed from the river. To the north, a golf course has been laid out, while beyond Puerto Madero there is now a substantial ecological reserve. Left wild to allow natural vegetation to grow and to attract birds and other wildlife, this nature reserve provides a picturesque contrast to the massive apartment buildings just across the way.

The Endless Pampas

The Río de la Plata sweeps on east past the city, widening still further until it pours into the Atlantic Ocean. Holidaying Argentines have to travel several hundred kilometres to the south of the river estuary to find sandy beaches for their vacations. For much of this distance, the banks of the river are largely flat and featureless. Behind them stretches the seemingly endless expanse of the grasslands that are the agricultural heartlands of Argentina. These pampas are richly fertile due to two factors: for millions of years, earth has been washed down from the Andes far to the west, creating deep deposits of alluvial soil. At the same time, they usually receive a reliable amount of rainfall of between 75 to 100 centimetres per year. In consequence, they are known as the *pampa humeda* or "wet pampa", as opposed to the drier *pampa seca* further south in Patagonia. This combination of conditions means that the grasslands can provide not only rich pasture land for huge herds of cattle, but are also ideal for the growing of crops, with wheat, maize and more recently soy beans all thriving.

Once again, the writer W. H. Hudson provides a memorable description of the pampas as they appeared to him as a young boy in the mid-1840s, recalled in old age in England:

> ... before us and on both sides the land, as far as one could see, was absolutely flat, everywhere green with the winter grass, but flowerless at that season, and with the gleam of water over the whole

expanse. It had been a season of great rains and much of the flat country had been turned into shallow lakes. That was all there was to see, except the herds of cattle and horses and an occasional horseman galloping over the plain, and the sight at long distances of a grove or small plantation of trees, marking the site of an estancia, or sheep and cattle farm, these groves appearing like islands on the sea-like flat country.

Hudson lived only a few kilometres outside Buenos Aires, in an area that has now been absorbed into the city. However, a century later, in 1945, the writer Florencio Escardó shows in his description of the same region that the city and countryside were still inextricably linked:

> ... the tremendous proximity of the city with the *pampa* is significant and instructive, and is possibly the most typical feature of Buenos Aires, a city of the plain. To reach the pampa, all any inhabitant of Buenos Aires has to do is to follow Avenida Saenz and before reaching the old Puente Alsina bridge, turn right along Avenida Coronel Roca; ten blocks further on, there is an impressive sight: the modest houses of the Nueva Pompeya neighbourhood are left behind, and the eyes are filled with the pampa itself, so typical, so immense and intense, still virgin, with no crops or tracks on it, but with marshes, lakes, bulrushes, grass, and the distant horizon. To the right stands the grove of trees round Flores cemetery, with in the distance the misty, smoky city. Between there and the onlooker are the Pereyra marshes, free of any stain of civilization apart from a brick kiln here and there, and a few adobe shacks and houses ... there is a strong sensation of being on a shore where there is none; the sweet-smelling grasses and the sweeping wind, ducks skimming over the land give a sense of distance that is hard to associate with the idea that one is only half an hour from Plaza de Mayo.

The pampas are most remarkable for their lack of definition, the absence of any outstanding geographical features or boundaries.

(On a visit in the 1930s, the French writer Pierre Drieu La Rochelle spoke of the sensation of "horizontal vertigo" they gave him). The city of Buenos Aires simply merges into this vast expanse. In the 1990s Alicia Dujovne Ortiz described this porous nature of the Argentine capital:

> Could you build a circular city on the pampas, a kernel-city, a city curled up like a tightened fist? Apparently not, since Buenos Aires is the epitome of expansiveness: the city pours itself out like a liquid. A city without boundaries ... I have always been astonished by those great cities of the world that have such precise boundaries that you can say exactly where they end. Buenos Aires has no end. It needs a beltway around it [the Avenida General Paz] so you could point an index finger, trembling with uncertainty, and say: 'You end up here. Up to this point, you are you. Beyond that, God only knows!'

As Dujovne Ortiz points out, it is only thanks to the artificial construction of the Avenida General Paz that the city of Buenos Aires is separated from its provincial suburbs (where nowadays more people live than in the Federal Capital itself). And her final exclamation, together with Escardó's mention of "civilization", highlights the idea that although there may be no physical boundary between Buenos Aires and the pampas, there is a clear symbolic one.

It was as recently as the 1870s that military campaigns finally destroyed the nomadic Indian groups that Schmidl had encountered more than three centuries earlier. For several hundred years, the southern boundary of "civilized" Argentina had been little more than a hundred kilometres from the city. Populated as it was by indigenous tribes and the mixed-race *gauchos* who were also seen as rejecting the "white man's" way of life, the pampas—the word *pampa* is Quechua for "plain"—were regarded as barbaric, a place to be shunned and avoided. In the 1870s the so-called "war of the desert" pushed the southern frontier of the Argentine nation ever further south into Patagonia. Yet despite promises made to the tens of thousands of European immigrants who began to flock to

Argentina that they would be given land of their own to farm, vast tracts were instead awarded to the military officers who had led the campaigns, or to already wealthy families in Buenos Aires. The result was that, almost always, the poor newcomers were forced to live and find work in the city and to forget their dreams of owning land and farms. These difficulties yet again reinforced the idea that the fertile grasslands so close by were somehow forbidden territory. The rich "oligarchy" built their *estancias* there—mansions in every imaginable style from French palaces to Edwardian mock-Tudor—and ran their estates from equally luxurious properties back in the civilised city. For all the other inhabitants of Buenos Aires, the pampas remained closed and hostile.

Paradoxically, the reality of being bounded on one side by a river with no further shore, and on most of the rest by the featureless pampas, can create a sense that Buenos Aires is hemmed in rather than opening out to the world. The Rio de la Plata emphasizes the truth that the city is perched on the edge of a huge continent: occasionally, when it is the stormy season hundreds of kilometres upstream, whole islands of greenery torn from the jungles go swirling past the skyscrapers of the city or anglers fishing for inedible fish, with bright green parakeets and even lost monkeys perched on their branches. Further downstream to the east is the vast, cold Atlantic Ocean, reminding the inhabitants of this port in the far south how distant they are from their roots, and creating an even greater feeling of loss and longing.

On the landward side, the flat pampas stretch out for hundreds of kilometres. Jorge Luis Borges was surely referring to this, as well as the apparently boundless river, in his 1929 poem "The Mythical Founding of Buenos Aires":

A tobacconist's perfumed the desert like a rose.
The evening drew in its yesterdays,
The men shared the illusion of a past.
Only one thing was missing: the other side of the street.

Although the pampas are nowadays crisscrossed by many roads, and no longer empty of people, still the only vertical features to be seen are the rusty wheels of wind pumps bringing water for the wandering herds of cattle, or the occasional oasis of eucalyptus or willow trees where a stream cuts through the endless plain. For centuries the fertile soil, which in many parts of the pampas is several metres deep, has meant that crops could grow and animals be fed without the need for fertilizers or intensive farming techniques. But in recent years, as the rains fail more frequently and crops such as genetically modified maize and, above all, soy bean for animal feed are increasingly being planted in areas previously left untouched, it appears that unless more thought is given to keeping the region's production sustainable, this natural bounty could finally be running out.

At the same time, to most city dwellers the *pampa* still seems to be a sort of no man's land, where they are unwelcome and ill at ease with only the distant horizon to look at. Far better to cross the flat lands as quickly as possible, either to reach the sea, the hills of Córdoba or the mountains of the Andes far to the west. Or to look inwards, and savour once more the chaotic diversity of the capital's streets.

The grid city, c.1760: a map by Jacques-Nicolas Bellin

2 | **The Urban Map**
Growth and Development

When Juan de Garay arrived with some sixty men and women to re-establish Buenos Aires in 1580, he brought with him a master plan for the city. In 1573 the Spanish emperor Felipe II had published his *Ordenanzas de Poblaciones*, regulations intended to bring some order to Spain's host of new possessions throughout the Americas. The model for the towns and cities springing up everywhere was based on a chequerboard design, with streets laid out in a straight line, and right-angled corners. This plan was intended to allow as much growth as might be necessary, always following the original layout. Buenos Aires was the last of the new cities to be established in the Río de la Plata region, and because of the lack of topographical constraints, it was ideally suited to the new imperial rules.

The main square or Plaza Mayor (now the Plaza de Mayo) was laid out behind the hilltop fortress. According to the regulations, "the main square should be no less than 28 metres wide by 84 metres long", and was to be surrounded by arcades "to offer facilities to the merchants established there". Twelve streets came off the square, one each from the centre of the four sides, and two from each corner. The imperial decree also stated that the main church should be built on the eastern side of the Plaza Mayor, "with a few steps up to it in order that it shall gain authority". The plaza was also intended to include the seat of government, a building for the town council, a jail and a hospital.

Copied from the ancient concept of the ideal city imposed during Rome's imperial conquests fifteen hundred years earlier, these regulations imposed a tight, logical structure on all the new conquests made by the Spanish crown. They are often seen as the most successful example of globalized "town planning" in history, and in Buenos Aires the original design still predominates in and around the capital's main square.

Juan de Garay's plan for the city beyond the Plaza Mayor was made up of a total of 144 blocks, separated by eleven streets. The limits of this first settlement were what are now Calle Viamonte to the north, Estados Unidos to the south and Libertad to the west. De Garay granted land titles to 232 people, each of whom were allotted a quarter of a block each; a Spanish woman, Ana Díaz, is said to have been the only woman to have been granted a property in this way. Beyond the grid of central streets, Garay also planned for large and small farms or *chacras* which could provide the settlement with fruit, vegetables and meat.

Despite the rigid equality of the planned outline, the richer and more important habitants of Buenos Aires had within a few years already mostly congregated in the south of the city, closer to the River Riachuelo and less exposed to attacks from the surrounding indigenous tribes. It was also on this side that the two main churches, the Basílica de la Merced (in Calle Reconquista) and the Convento de Santo Domingo (also still in existence) were built.

At the end of the sixteenth century, twenty years on from de Garay's successful foundation of the city, the population of Buenos Aires is thought to have been around 1,100 people. (At this same period Potosí, the city built round the "mountain of silver" discovered in Bolivia, could boast more than 120,000 inhabitants). The early city dwellers in this southern port were a mixture of people who came directly from Spain (*peninsulares*), as well as *criollos* from other parts of Argentina or South America. They already included merchants, soldiers and imperial clerks, as well as farmers and labourers. In 1617 the city was given a further boost when it was named capital of the Province of Río de la Plata, followed shortly afterwards by the appointment of a bishop and the establishment of a Royal audience. Apart from the river commerce, the first licences for people to own cattle were issued, giving a further impulse to trade.

With Buenos Aires growing in importance as Argentina's outlet towards Europe on the Atlantic, the cities in the interior such as Tucumán, Salta or Córdoba sought to limit its ability to trade through the richer Spanish possessions of Bolivia and Peru. This tussle for influence was a continuing factor over the next two centuries, and eventually led to armed conflict once the country as a whole had won independence from Spain.

In the seventeenth century, Spain was still trying to force all trade back to Europe to go through its ports in Peru and Mexico. This meant that Buenos Aires grew only slowly, its wealth based on contraband silver exports from Bolivia as well as hides and tallow from the pampas. In 1680, a hundred years after its founding, the population was probably no more than 5,000. Among those classified as foreign, the Portuguese were by far the most numerous, while the wealthiest were those who had come directly from Spain.

Most of these inhabitants lived in one storey dwellings made of adobe, with straw or occasionally red-tiled roofs; in this horizontal cityscape, the church towers stood out above everything else. It is said to have been the Jesuits, influential in Argentina from the early seventeenth century, who discovered how to make bricks from the local earth. It was the Jesuits, too, who used stone to build their baroque San Ignacio Church in 1713 (on Calle Bolívar), the oldest surviving construction in the centre of Buenos Aires, which is also famous for the maze of tunnels running underneath it.

Between 1580 and the end of the seventeenth century, the population grew by fifty per cent as Buenos Aires increasingly became a regional centre for European imports. In the early 1670s trade between Buenos Aires and ships from Holland, France and Britain had grown to such an extent that the Spanish monarch Carlos II wrote to his subjects in Buenos Aires explaining how trade with foreign countries weakened Spain, and rebuking colonial officials in the port for getting rich on contraband goods. The least savoury commerce was in black slaves from Africa.

Spain was forbidden by the 1494 Treaty of Tordesillas to trade with Africa, and so *asientos* or licences were issued to the Portuguese to bring slaves across the Atlantic. (These *asientos* were sold to the highest bidder, with the proceeds going to the Spanish crown.) By the eighteenth century it was the British who began to control trade with the distant colonial outpost. In 1713, thanks to the Treaty of Utrecht that ended the War of the Spanish Succession, Britain was given the contract to supply 4,800 African slaves per year to the Spanish colonies in the Americas. This contract was handed on to the private South Seas Company, which quickly established a warehouse and offices in Buenos Aires. According to some authors, as the eighteenth century wore on it was not uncommon for one rich white family to have up to forty black slaves, working either as domestic servants or in agriculture.

By 1750 some 14,000 people were living in Buenos Aires, most of them devoted to commerce or helping administer the Spanish imperial system. The local cattle owners and merchants gradually acquired considerable wealth and status, and the city became a magnet for European fashions in everything from dress to cooking utensils. Mostof these goods were produced in the newly-industrializing countries of northern Europe rather than Spain. The rich and influential inhabitants built grander houses as close to the centre of the city as possible, with landowners living side by side with merchants.

By the second half of the eighteenth century, the Spanish empire was crumbling, and its hold on its territories in Latin America was loosening. In a desperate attempt at reform of the imperial system, the authorities in Spain in 1776 recognized the growing importance of Buenos Aires. By royal decree, the city became the capital of the newly-established Viceroyalty of the Río de la Plata, thus freeing it from subordination to Lima. In 1778 this move was followed by a Free Trade Law, which allowed the city to export and import goods with other countries in addition to Spain. Following these moves, the first Viceroy of the Río de la Plata, Don Juan José de Vértiz y Salcedo (1777-84), embarked on an ambitious plan to improve the city.

It was under his energetic management that Buenos Aires began to change from a low, hilltop village into a city with neoclassical stone buildings that housed new institutions. A school, the Colegio de San Carlos, was charged with bringing the lessons of the Enlightenment to this southern outpost. The first printing press was set up, while oil lamps were placed along the central avenue or Alameda. The Calle Florida became the first paved street outside the main Plaza Mayor. A theatre, the Casa de Comedias, was built, it was here that in 1789 *Siripo*, the first Argentine-authored tragedy, was performed. A naval school was set up to help train young men for the growing commerce with the outside world.

By the turn of the nineteenth century, the city had grown to fill the newly-reclaimed land around Retiro in the north, to Calle Patricios in San Telmo to the south, and in the west as far as what is now Callao-Entre Ríos. According to urban historian D. J. Keeling, Buenos Aires could now be seen as comprising four distinct areas: the first, the civic centre round the Plaza Mayor; the second, a wealthier neighbourhood to the south, down to the Riachuelo. Then there was a ring of eight churches, showing how important the Catholic religion was to colonial society, each of them the focal point of a parish. Finally, on the outskirts of the city lay a less densely popu-lated area "where proto-industrial activities (brickworks, tileworks, lime kilns) mixed with small stores, open areas for cart storage, and small orchards and farms".

Such growth notwithstanding, the Buenos Aires of the years of the struggle for independence from Spain at the start of the nine-teenth century was still a small, cramped place with narrow streets mostly of one-storey buildings clustered by the river. The streets were narrow enough for the inhabitants to pour boiling water and excrement down on the British troops who invaded the city in 1806 and again in the following year, and to make the city dangerous enough for the invaders to beat a hasty retreat.

It was also at the start of the nineteenth century that the Plaza Mayor was redesigned, with the construction of the Recova, a big central market for meat, fruit and other foodstuffs. This market lasted for almost seventy years, although an Argentine doctor of the time, Eduardo Wilde, had his doubts about how hygienic it might be: "the two rows of stalls in the Recova were almost all given over to clothes shops, usually of rather low quality. It was mainly sailors who bought there . . . and the shop-keepers would all eat there. They were brought their food in tin containers, so that between two and three in the afternoon you could not walk through the market be-cause the smell of food was unbearable. The stench coming out of each shop in summer was so strong it felled you like a gunshot. No-one who was in the habit of walking through the Recova in those days will ever forget its *sui generis* smell."

The Recova was one of the outstanding features in the centre of the city until its demolition was ordered by Torcuato de Alvear, the first *intendente* (mayor) of what by the 1880s had become Argentina's federal capital. This was part of his grand plan to make Buenos Aires a more open and spacious city. Several hundred work-men pulled the market down in a single day; the small but famous statue known as the Pirámide de Mayo was moved to its present position next to the Casa Rosada, while formal gardens replaced the foul-smelling markets stalls.

Independence

Buenos Aires had been in the forefront of the battle to win inde-pendence from Spain. The city council or *cabildo* first declared its refusal to recognize rule from the peninsula on 25 May 1810. The members of the council were pressured into this decision by the crowds of *porteños* and the local militias congregated outside the building in the city centre. This was the start of a long tradition of ordinary people filling the main square to support or threaten the politicians inside, a tradition which has given the Plaza Mayor (later renamed Plaza de Mayo in honour of the revolutionary proclamation of 1810) huge symbolic significance for the whole of Argentina. The armed struggles of the following years mostly took place far from the capital, although in 1813 the revolutionary leaders staged a spectacular burning of torture instruments after the Constitutional Assembly declared an end to the Inquisition. Further revolutionary measures included freedom to all the children of slaves and abol-ishing all titles of nobility. When the Spanish armies were finally defeated and the independence of the new nation of Argentina was declared in 1816, Buenos Aires became increasingly important as the entrance and exit port for trade with Europe. The proceeds of this exchange stayed largely in the city, however, which meant that the struggle for dominance within the newly-independent country grew more critical. The older centres of influence in the middle of the country and the north rebelled against the increasing wealth and power of Buenos Aires, especially during the dictatorship of Juan Manuel de Rosas, which lasted from 1835 to 1852. Charles Darwin, who met the dictator when he stopped off in the Argentine capital during his epic voyage on *The Beagle*, described the city of his day in these terms:

> The city of Buenos Ayres is large some 60,000 people and I should think one of the most regular in the world. Every street is at right angles to the one it crosses, and the parallel ones being equidistant, the houses are collected into solid squares of equal dimensions, which are called *quadras*. On the other hand, the houses themselves are hollow squares; all the rooms opening into a neat little courtyard. They are generally only one story high, with flat roofs, which are fitted with seats and are much frequented by the inhabitants in summer. In the centre of the town is the Plaza, where the public offices, fortress, cathedral, etc., stand. Here also, the old viceroys, before the revolution, had their palaces. The general assemblage of buildings possesses considerable architectural beauty, although none individually can boast of any.

In the years following independence, the city continued its gradual development. The year 1821 saw the creation of the famous Recoleta cemetery in what until then had been the gardens of the Recoleto Fathers, an Augustinian order, alongside the Basílica de Nuestra Señora del Pilar, to the north of the city centre. A year later, President Bernardo de Rivadavia wrote for the first time of the need for an avenue encircling the city to define its boundaries: his project roughly followed the line of what today is the Avenida Callao. Even so, during the first half of the nineteenth century, the expansion of Buenos Aires was largely restricted. There was little local industry, as Britain and the other already industrialized countries preferred to keep Argentina as a market for their goods rather than encourage manufacturing there.

British ships continued to bring in finished goods, and returned to Europe with Argentina's agricultural riches in their holds. The first British diplomat in Buenos Aires after its recognition of the newly independent nation, the picturesquely named Sir Woodbine Parish, noted that even the gauchos out on the pampas had by now become part of this global trading system: "take his whole equipment, examine everything about him—and what is there not of hide that is not British? If his wife has a gown, ten to one it is from Manchester. The camp kettle in which he cooks his food, the common earthenware he eats from, his knife, spoon, bits and the poncho which covers him, are all imported from England."

At the same time, it was the British who took a leading role in bringing services and up-to-date communications to the growing city.

The 1850s saw the appearance of the first railway lines built by British companies, which brought with them urban development around the new stations and commuter lines. By the early 1860s, these lines had spread as far as the Tigre Delta in the north, Moreno in the west and out towards the town of La Plata to the south-east. The 1870s witnessed the growth of a horse-drawn tram network. This and the railways further encouraged the spread of the city, thus diluting the concentration of buildings and inhabitants around the central square that had predominated for almost three hundred years.

Argentina held its first national census in 1869, when the struggles for political dominance between the provinces and the capital had finally been resolved in favour of the latter. The census showed that the greater Buenos Aires area could by now boast almost 200,000 inhabitants, while the country's total population stood at fewer than two million. According to the census, Buenos Aires in 1869 still had 1,300 dwellings with straw roofs. By the time of the following census in 1895, such buildings had diminished to 196 (one of the landmarks to disappear in this period was the founder Juan de Garay's house on the Plaza de Mayo), while in less than thirty years the population of the city had grown by more than 250 per cent.

By the time of the 1910 centenary celebrations of the declaration of independence from Spain, the equivalent figures were almost a million inhabitants in the city, and some four million in the country as a whole. Thanks to its exports of meat, grain and wool, Argentina had become one of the ten wealthiest economies in the world, while Buenos Aires was not only the largest city in Latin America, but was second only in size to New York in the entire continent.

The main factor in this development from the second half of the nineteenth century onwards was massive immigration from Europe. This lasted for close to a century until after the Second World War. "To govern is to populate," was President Juan Bautista Alberdi's slogan as early as the 1850s, and this policy was keenly followed by his successors. Although the newly-arrived immigrants were promised a job and land to farm, the vast majority soon discovered that the rich farming lands of the pampas already had owners, who were unwilling to welcome newcomers except as seasonal labourers. This forced almost all the immigrants back into the city of Buenos Aires, where many subsequently started the small-scale artisan businesses that have been a prominent feature of the city to the present day.

As in earlier centuries, it was the area to the south of the Plaza de Mayo that continued to be the most prestigious and prosperous neighbourhood. Around the Riachuelo in Barracas, the meat salting industry continued to grow, along with warehouses for cattle and sheep hides. However, in 1870 and 1871, there were two major outbreaks of yellow fever in this part of the city. This led to an exodus of the wealthiest two hundred families to the northern outskirts around Belgrano, Palermo and what is still seen as the most stylish part of the city, the Barrio Norte (northern neighbourhood). The rich *porteños* did not seem to mind that their expensive mansions were often grouped around or close to the Recoleta cemetery. This population shift was also encouraged by the fact that the newly-emerging banks were situated north of the central square, as was the main paved shopping street, Calle Florida, which ran north from Avenida de Mayo and was home to many of the city's wealthiest families.

This expansion of the city was aided by the vision and enthusiasm of President Domingo Faustino Sarmiento (1868-74). During his many years in exile, Sarmiento had visited Europe and lived in the United States, and was determined to bring the benefits of the material progress he had seen there back to the Argentine capital. He personally oversaw work on the first sewerage and running water systems, as well as the building of the iconic Post and Telegraph office in El Bajo, from where Argentina's first postal system and telegraph network were created. President Sarmiento was also responsible for converting the marshy ground in the north of the city into the Parque Tres de Febrero (now Palermo), often regarded as the Bois de Boulogne of Buenos Aires. He also brought many varieties of trees from Europe and Japan to line the city's newly-created avenues.

His pioneering work in this respect was continued by Jules Charles Thays. A Frenchman, he arrived in Argentina in 1889 and throughout the 1890s was responsible for the planting of many of the exuberant trees along the central streets, as well as designing parks such as Parque Lezama, Parque Patricios and Parque Centenario, in addition to public squares like Constitución and Congreso. Perhaps more than anyone, Thays helped Buenos Aires acquire its fame as the "Paris of South America". His crowning achievement was the Jardín Botánico (Botanical Garden of Buenos Aires), which still boasts an impressive collection of the native plants of Argentina, and offers several hectares of quiet, shady greenery in the north of the city. Often the loudest noise in the garden comes from the roaming gangs of semi-feral cats, which continue to thrive and multiply despite repeated appeals by the authorities for *porteños* not to feed them and not to dump their own pets there when they have had enough of them.

As the richer inhabitants moved northwards to the salubrious suburbs, the properties near the docks and warehouses in the south became filled with the families of the European immigrants who by the second half of the nineteenth century were disembarking in their thousands each year in the booming port. Although some areas of La Boca close to the river are nowadays considered as picturesque tourist attractions, in the late 1800s many of the district's streets were comprised of miserable tin and wooden shacks with poor sanitation and few facilities. Some of the other previously grand mansions were divided into family units known as *conventillos*, similar to the tenements of New York or other big US cities.

Capital Status

It was in 1880 that the city of Buenos Aires was named the federal capital of Argentina. The city itself occupied almost 19,000 hectares, with beyond it the province of Buenos Aires. In 1887 the municipalities of Belgrano and Flores were ceded from the province to the capital city, and they still mark the outer limits of the city. These were the first middle-class commuter neighbourhoods, inhabited by clerks, civil servants and many of the British managers and employees who ran the railways and the public utilities. Even today there are odd corners in the neighbourhoods of Flores or Caballito that would not look out of place in a suburb of London, as the Argentine writer Ernesto Schóo wrote of a part of the Caballito neighbourhood as recently as 2011:

> If you turn right into Calle Videla, go on a couple of blocks and suddenly, like Alice entering into Wonderland, you are in Victorian London. But however much you rub your eyes, the miracle is still there, it's concrete, real. Four blocks of typical Victorian two-storey mansions, tiled roofs, porticos with columns, bow windows, gardens out the front. White, immaculate, perfect, all exactly the same.

It is not hard, Mary Poppins-style, to imagine the English bank employees setting out from here on the modern trams of the 1880s, heading for the financial centre or "La City" of Buenos Aires, a district which occupies three or four blocks just north of the Plaza de Mayo. However, such examples of a surviving architectural past are increasingly rare. In recent years speculative development in these sought-after neighbourhoods has led to the disappearance of historic low-rise buildings in favour of tower blocks of apartments that are often left empty, and do little to resolve the capital's chronic housing problems.

Torcuato de Alvear was the city's first mayor (1880-87) after it became the federal capital. Like Sarmiento before him, he had visited Europe and was determined to model the new capital on Paris, where he had been highly impressed with the modernization undertaken by Baron Haussmann. The nineteenth-century French ideal of open, airy avenues replaced the tightly-enclosed, rigid Spanish design. Torcuato de Alvear opened up the Plaza de Mayo to create the Avenida de Mayo. This avenue duly became the fulcrum for the city. It divided the capital into north and south, and eventually came to link the Casa Rosada, the president's office, with the grandiose national parliament building of the Congreso (finished in 1906 and modelled on the Capitol building in Washington DC) some two kilometres to the west of the executive seat of power.

The Avenida de Mayo was where the first automobiles appeared in the city in the 1890s, and where the first underground railway or "Subte" was built as early as 1913 by the Anglo-Argentine Underground Company. This company was granted the concession for Buenos Aires' first three underground lines for the remarkable period of eighty years. It was later deemed to have broken the terms of the contract, however, and in 1936 the lines were taken over by the Corporación del Transporte de Buenos Aires. The original company appealed against the decision, and won its case—and the city of Buenos Aires only finally finished paying off its £7 million debt to the company in 1981.

Close beside the new Subte station in Avenida de Mayo, the Café de la Victoria and the Café Tortoni were already well-known social landmarks, while the avenue and its adjoining streets came to house large theatres and the very first cinemas. Further broad avenues were opened up by tearing down many of the original city buildings to create the three other main thoroughfares that run parallel to the Avenida de Mayo: Santa Fe, Córdoba and Corrientes. The rectangle formed by these four avenues and the *centro* is still regarded as the heart of the capital. At the start of Santa Fe, running from the Plaza San Martín to the financial district, stands Calle Florida, for many years the artistic centre and luxury shopping street. Famous names such as Harrods of London, Lalique and Tiffany had stores here for the wealthy clientele living nearby, and there were furriers and jewellers as well as exclusive clubs, restaurants and cafés. Further west an entertainment district grew up, with the neoclassical Teatro Colón for opera and ballet-lovers at one end, and the theatres and cinemas on Avenida Corrientes and Lavalle at the other. A further kilometre west, around Plaza Once, was the "rag-trade" area, with many wholesale and cheap retail clothes outlets.

Some of the most prosperous inhabitants constructed French style mansions: the old land-owning families and the newcomers who became rich through trade soon became known as the "oligarchy" in a country that had thrown off the Spanish monarchy. The city itself was no longer recognizably Spanish-looking, as more and more immigrants from Italy, Germany, the Ukraine and other parts of Eastern Europe and the Middle East continued to pour in year after year, bringing their own customs and building styles with them.

Metropolis

Between 1880 and 1930 Buenos Aires grew in an almost chaotic fashion. The cities and regions of the interior now served almost exclusively to serve the capital. Buenos Aires was where political power and wealth increasingly came to be concentrated. Foreign capital and businesses were attracted to the port city, to the detriment of the rest of the country. It was in this period that Buenos Aires became what one writer termed "a Goliath's head on a puny body". It has been calculated that in the early years of the twentieth century, 25 per cent of Argentina's manufacturing capacity was based in the city or its outskirts, some 30 per cent of all Argentines employed in industrial activities lived there, and over half of industrial investments (led at this time by the British) were focussed on the city. This increasing domination consolidated the rift between the *porteños* and those living in the provinces, with the former often regarding the latter as slow and retrograde in their views, whilst the latter returned the compliment by viewing the inhabitants of the capital as vain, over-sophisticated and not truly "Latin American".

Typical of the domination of Buenos Aires over the rest of the country was the way that the railway system fanned out from the capital. Although many of the public buildings built in this period were based on French or North American models, the vast new railway stations constructed in the early twentieth century followed British examples. Retiro station, its lines leading out north up the estuary of the Río de la Plata, was built in 1913 by engineers from Liverpool, while the other great station at Constitución was modelled on London's Victoria station. By the early twentieth century, the Argentina railway network covered almost 40,000 kilometres, with Buenos Aires at its centre, receiving not only beef and mutton in its refrigerated plants (also owned by the British), but also wool, minerals, and grain that then moved to the capital's docks. The railway also brought passengers from all over the vast country.

Between first census of 1869 and the third carried out in 1914, the population of Buenos Aires and greater Buenos Aires had grown to more than two million, a tenfold increase in 45 years. Already in 1869, some seventy per cent of these inhabitants were first generation immigrants, and this proportion grew still further during the early years of the twentieth century. Housing all these new arrivals became an increasing problem; according to the 1914 census, approximately four out of five working-class families lived in one room.

In the 1920s Buenos Aires was comprised of four main areas. The financial and administrative centre, in what was known as "La City", was still grouped around the historic centre. The Barrio Norte, Palermo and further out Belgrano (where many German immigrants settled) were neighbourhoods for the well-off. Beyond them lay the greener suburbs of San Isidro, Olivos (where the presidential residence is situated) and other small towns along the riverbank of the Río de la Plata, with *quintas* or villas stretching out towards the Tigre Delta. (These areas are still favoured by many expatriate businessmen and their wives, as well as wealthy Argentines; here the sports played are rugby, hockey and polo rather than football). To the south, around the Riachuelo, lay the working-class areas of La Boca, Barracas, Avellaneda and Nueva Pompeya, where the dock-workers and all those employed in industries related to agricultural products tended to live, and further west, the aptly-named Mataderos neighbourhood contained the main slaughterhouses for the cattle and sheep from the pampas, as well as the huge municipal rubbish dump in Nueva Chicago.

Even with such rapid and often unplanned growth, Buenos Aires liked to style itself the Paris of South America, and considered itself as on a par architecturally with the capitals of Europe. But when one of the most famous contemporary European architects, the Swiss-French Henri Le Corbusier, came on a visit in 1929, he was dismayed by what he found: "Buenos Aires is one of the most inhuman cities I have known; really, one's heart is martyred. For weeks I walked its streets, 'without hope' like a madman, oppressed, depressed, furious, desperate." At the same time, the city excited him: "Nevertheless, where does one feel as here such a potential of energy, such power, the strong and tireless pressure of an inevitable destiny?" It was Le Corbusier, too, who is said to have dubbed Buenos Aires "the capital of an imaginary empire". In his drawings and reflections on his trip there, he hoped to convert it from a dark, congested series of corridors into a more open city that reconnected with the river and its huge sky.

Nothing ever came of Le Corbusier's plans for turning Buenos Aires into a modernist utopia. Instead, the city continued to expand during the 1930s in a more or less haphazard fashion, with no master plan. Much of the new construction was concentrated on a road network: the ambitious scheme to construct a beltway separating the federal capital from the province was finally achieved when the Avenida General Paz was completed in 1941. This took cars and lorries from the port area in the south to the northern suburbs without the need to go through the centre of the city, but as with many major projects its success caused unexpected problems. By the end of the 1970s, the amount of traffic using the avenue and its feeder roads was so great, especially at weekends when tens of thousands of city dwellers sought to escape to the countryside for at least a few hours, that it often became clogged with kilometre after kilometre of stationary traffic vehicles.

Unlike many of the European cities to which the inhabitants of the Argentine capital liked to compare it, Buenos Aires was fortunate not to suffer the ravages of the Second World War. As a result it enjoys a continuity of building styles from nineteenth-century grandeur to modernism and beyond, even if lack of planning means that they are often in violent juxtaposition.

Further schemes were carried out in the 1930s which dramatically altered the central part of the city. The most striking of these is the Avenida 9 de Julio, so called in honour of the day of definitive independence from Spain in 1816. Often hailed by proud *porteños* as the "widest avenue in the world", it links Retiro station in the north-west of the city with Constitución to the south-east. (Buenos Aires also boasts "the longest avenue in the world", Avenida Rivadavia, which extends Avenida de Mayo from the Congreso westwards for some 35 kilometres). To allow construction of Avenida 9 de Julio in 1935, a swathe of buildings a block wide was demolished all along its two kilometres' length. (Only the French refused to have their elegant embassy pulled down, and it still stands rather incongruously among the traffic at the northern end of the avenue just above Retiro station.) Gardens were planted in the middle, and no fewer than seven lanes of traffic were allowed in each direction. At the centre of the avenue is perhaps the most recognizable of Buenos Aires' monuments: the Obelisk, built in 1936 at the intersection of 9 de Julio and Avenida Corrientes to commemorate the fourth centenary of the city's first foundation by Pedro de Mendoza.

The flow of immigrants from Europe slackened in the 1950s, but their place was increasingly taken by migrants from the interior and poorer neighbouring countries such as Bolivia and Paraguay. The populist governments under General Juan Domingo Perón (from 1946 to 1955) encouraged this tendency, as the newly emerging national industries were concentrated in and around the capital. Thanks to Perón and his wife Evita, the first high-rise apartment blocks for workers were built on the outskirts of the city. However, the pressure of new arrivals also meant that *villas miseria* or shanty towns began to spring up, either close to railway and bus stations such as Retiro, or on the periphery of the capital on the other side of the Avenida General Paz.

After the Second World War capital investment from the United States replaced earlier British finance. This led to the expansion of a second industrial belt in the outer municipalities. As a result the population of the metropolis continued to grow, from just under five million in 1947 to some fourteen million in 2010 (when the national population was put at forty million) but most of this increase has been in the area beyond the Avenida General Paz, while the population of the federal capital itself has slightly decreased, to a little less than three million.

The continuing dominance of Buenos Aires over the other regions of Argentina has led to repeated calls for greater efforts be made to transfer shipping, industry and public sector workers elsewhere. In the mid-1980s President Raúl Alfonsín even suggested that the federal capital should be transferred almost a thousand kilometres south to the small town of Viedma in Patagonia. While this idea made sense on a rational level, no-one in Argentina, and particularly in Buenos Aires, ever saw this vast upheaval as a real possibility. As it is, the capital still accounts for some eighty per cent of Argentina's imports, a third of its exports and nearly all its ministries and administrative headquarters, as well as playing a pre-eminent role in its social and cultural life.

Within the city, the political and economic upheavals of the past forty years have also left their mark. There has been inadequate investment in infrastructure and social welfare. The typical *porteño* middle classes have found their lifestyle under threat, and there has been increased tension between differing social classes forced to live cheek-by-jowl. The city's environment has worsened as private cars have steadily replaced public transport. Life in the city's *barrios*, which often even until very recently still revolved around the local public market, the corner fruit and vegetable store, the kiosk for buying newspapers and confectionery, the neighbourhood pharmacy, the café and *boliche* (an unassuming restaurant where you could eat for little more than it would cost to make a meal at home), has come under mounting pressure. Shopping malls have replaced the familiar stores, and raised freeways have cut through the centre of the city. Several of these were begun during the military dictatorships from 1976 to 1983, when many buildings in the city centre were demolished to make way for them. These projects, known scornfully by *porteños* as *obras faraónicas* (pharaonic works), were left uncompleted when the military governments ended, but have gradually come into service in more recent years.

The central Avenida 9 de Julio, for example, has been connected to elevated toll roads leading out to the city's international airport and the west of greater Buenos Aires, as well as to routes to the cities of La Plata and Mar del Plata further down the coast. These highways provide any new arrival to the city from the main airport with a startling view of the densely built cityscape. The city's international airport, some forty kilometres to the west of the capital, is officially named after General Juan Pistarini, but is more commonly known as Ezeiza, after the village close to which it was built in the second half of the 1940s. (Ezeiza shares with Entebbe airport in Uganda the unhappy privilege of also being commonly known as the site of a massacre. It was here in 1973 that rival factions among the one million people who had come to welcome General Perón back to Argentina following eighteen years in exile started a shootout that left as many as a hundred dead, while the returning leader was forced to land at a nearby small military airport instead.)

While Ezeiza was built to serve international flights, the Aeroparque Jorge Newbery was constructed at around the same time to deal with domestic air traffic and for the short hop across the Río de la Plata to Uruguay. Unlike Ezeiza, however, Aeroparque was situated almost in the middle of the city, close to the riverside *costanera* and the bank of the Río de la Plata. As the airport has become busier and busier, there have been repeated attempts to move it to a safer and quieter location, possibly on a man-made island out in the river. None of these plans has prospered, however, and planes still come skimming in dangerously over the river, the heavy traffic of Avenida Libertador and the green spaces of Palermo every few minutes.

The Modern City

In the twenty-first century, Buenos Aires continues to grow and change. First there has been the return to the riverside at Puerto Madero. The redevelopment of the old docks has quickly made this one of the most sought-after parts of the city, with upmarket apartments in towers up to fifty storeys high commanding views over both the Río de la Plata and the rest of the city centre. Restaurants, a huge new art gallery and several international hotels have changed the face of the city yet again.

The other new development has been the advent of gated communities outside the capital. This move has been spurred on because residents of previously quiet suburban areas have found themselves living in close proximity with some of the poorest communities in greater Buenos Aires. In response, those who can afford to have migrated to new, more secure "urban centres" still further out, connected to the city centre by the high-speed freeways. (One commentator has pointed out how similar these new creations are to the tiny, beleaguered fortress that Pedro de Mendoza built almost five centuries ago.) For example, a sixteen-lane highway leads north out of the city to Nordelta, the largest gated community in Latin America. Situated close to the Tigre Delta, according to its prospectus Nordelta offers:

> An avenue surrounded by palms. Great green areas and parks. Lime trees, spruces, willow-trees and magnolias. An enormous and silent water surface. And everything, that design and comfort could nowadays introduce to achieve a better life. A place like this does exist. And it is not at the end of the world. It is exactly in the geographical centre of Nordelta. Its name is *The Island*.

So says the 2002 publicity brochure intended to attract *porteños* to this development, planned eventually to house some 80,000 people. It will include a huge shopping mall, a civic centre and a private university as well as several private schools through its thirty "neighbourhoods". To emphasize how secure Nordelta is meant to be, the publicity material boasts that emergency vehicles can reach any major point in the new community within less than two minutes.

Not everyone in Buenos Aires is happy about this kind of expansion. In fact, what distinguishes the city from many other capitals in Latin America (Lima, Bogota, Mexico City and so on) as well as North American post-industrial cities is that the historic centre is still very much inhabited. Not only do thousands of commuters come into its "City" every day, but middle-class people choose to live as close as possible to the Obelisk, the Plaza de Mayo or even the Riachuelo. Buenos Aires may not be a utopia, but its streets and great buildings are still a powerful magnet.

THE URBAN MAP

35

The French-influenced, neoclassical Edificio Bencich, an apartment block
built in 1927 (Elsapucai/Wikimedia Commons)

3 | Landmarks
Buildings and Styles

lthough Buenos Aires was founded more than four hundred years ago, there are very few buildings left that reflect the Spanish colonial heritage. Nor are there any known architectural remains from the pre-Hispanic era. The heart of the old city in and around the Plaza Mayor (nowadays Plaza de Mayo) has nearly all been torn down and replaced in the course of the nineteenth and twentieth centuries. Unlike in Mexico or Peru, the Spanish colonizers of the Río de la Plata did not encounter a flourishing indigenous civilization whose architecture they could build on (often quite literally), while the relative lack of importance and wealth in Buenos Aires during the colonial period meant there were no grandiose cathedrals, gold-bedecked baroque churches or even imposing civil buildings.

The original fortress constructed by Juan de Garay in 1580 was pulled down in the nineteenth century, judged to be too small and unworthy of the expanding, dynamic city. The current government house or Casa Rosada (the "Pink House" in opposition to Washington's White House) was built on its site. Designed by Swedish architects as two separate buildings, they were joined together in 1879 to form one squat warren of offices and courtyards. By far the most important and symbolic aspect of this largely unprepossessing building is the first-floor balcony that gives directly onto the Plaza de Mayo in front of it. It was there that in October 1945 thousands of workers assembled, demanding the release of the then Colonel Perón from prison. After his election to the presidency the following year, Juan Domingo Perón and his second wife Evita, masters of the use of the media and the manipulation of crowds of supporters, began to appear on this balcony in the late 1940s and early 1950s to appeal directly to their massed followers in the square. As Jason Wilson points out, the plaza "symbolizes the place where a populist, national unity can be re-enacted". The tenor of those speeches and the way in which Peronism did not so much unify the nation as draw up battle-lines can be gathered from the following short extract from the speech that Evita gave from the balcony on Labour Day, 1 May 1953, a year before her death:

> Friends: when this morning General Perón finished his victory message, he said that triumph belonged to the fatherland and to the people; that it was ours, and only ours. And I thought what you must have thought: that if it wasn't for Perón, we would be back in the old First of May celebrations put on by the oligarchy to weep over our dead rather than to celebrate victory.
>
> We agree with you, my general, that the triumph belongs to the fatherland and to the people. We agree that as workers, as humble people, we have always been on our feet and have embraced just causes—and that is why we embrace the cause of Perón. But what would have become of the fatherland and of the workers without Perón? That is why we give thanks to God that he has given us the privilege of having Perón, of knowing Perón, of understanding him, loving him, and following Perón.

The military leaders who overthrew Perón in 1955 caused panic and outrage when their aeroplanes bombed and strafed the square, causing hundreds of casualties in what they called the "Liberating Revolution". The unelected governments that followed, and in particular the military junta which seized power in 1976 and launched a "dirty war" that led to the torture, death and disappearance of many thousands of Argentines, were only too well aware of the symbolism of the square and the presidential balcony. They shied well away from public appearances there, until the junta's leader General Leopoldo Fortunato Galtieri embarked on the "heroic deed" of invading the Malvinas/Falklands Islands in April 1982. He soon came out drunkenly on to the balcony to receive the acclaim of the thousands of his countrymen packed into the square below. Barely a couple of months later, many of the same people returned, howling for Galtieri and his military cohorts to get out.

The same happened in the 1980s following the return of civilian government. When it appeared that a military revolt might overthrow the elected authorities, thousands of *porteños* packed the square to defend their elected representatives. At the end of 2001 they were back to do just the opposite: sickened by corruption and political mismanagement, huge crowds gathered in the square demanding that the president and all corrupt politicians pack their bags and go. Eventually President Fernando de la Rúa was forced to make a rapid exit from the presidential palace in a helicopter. Nowadays there is rarely the same political fervour in Buenos Aires, although the Peronists can still bus in thousands of their faithful for rallies in the square.

Facing the Casa Rosada stands the small pyramid that commemorates the 1810 "revolution", but perhaps the most poignant feature is a circle of flagstones bearing the white image of head-scarves. These were first worn by the mothers and grandmothers of those Argentines who were "disappeared" by agents of the state between 1976 and 1983, women who defied persecution and the threat of their own abduction to march round the square every Thursday in silent protest. (Memorials against state barbarity have sprung up throughout Buenos Aires, with bronze plaques on pavements in several places that mark the spot where victims were kidnapped by the security forces in those dark days.)

The Casa Rosada is flanked by the city's cathedral, and opposite it stands the *cabildo*, the original seat of the city government (and its first prison). The cathedral is a disappointing mishmash of early nineteenth-century pomposity; perhaps the most interesting element is the recently-restored side chapel that contains the remains of the great national hero General José de San Martín, who could not be buried inside the cathedral because he was a freemason. Nor is the *cabildo* architecturally inspiring: it has been rebuilt many times since its first incarnation in the mid-eighteenth century, and its rough white exterior and tower are now engulfed by the much taller buildings all around it.

Little is left either of the original Spanish colonial churches. It was the Jesuit Order which first began making baked bricks in the city at the end of the seventeenth century, and the Jesuits soon began to use them to replace the less durable adobe constructions. The Jesuit Church of San Ignacio Loyola (at Calle Bolívar 225), built near the main square between 1712 and 1734, is regarded as the oldest surviving place of worship in the city. Designed by the Bavarian Jesuit Juan Kraus, it has a baroque façade and a Latin-cross outline, with a fine seventeenth-century wooden altarpiece. None of the remaining colonial churches in the Argentine capital can offer any of the splendours to be found in Mexico or Peru.

However, it is another monument that many *porteños* and provincial Argentines visiting the capital as tourists see as both the centre of the city and its most powerful symbol. This is the seventy-metre tall obelisk, which dominates the central Avenida 9 de Julio where it intersects with Avenida Corrientes. It was built in under two months in1936 by a German company to commemorate 400 years since the city's first foundation. Like so much of modern Buenos Aires, its construction involved the loss of a symbol of the city's historical and architectural heritage: in this case, the demolition of the church where the first national flag was kept. The obelisk's simple modernist lines and gleaming white stone soon turned it into one of the iconic sights of the city—with many jokes about its phallic nature passing into local folklore. The Obelisk has not been without its detractors, though. In 1938, barely two years after its inauguration, the city council ordered its demolition on public safety and aesthetic grounds, but this decision was overturned by the executive, who argued that it had already become part of Argentina's national heritage. Further controversy arose in the early 1970s because of the huge slogan the Peronist government under Isabel Martínez de Perón put round the base of the monument. Although they claimed that the slogan *El silencio es salud* (Silence is Health) was aimed at noisy drivers, the *porteños* soon saw this as a threat to their right to speak openly: a threat that all too quickly became a reality when the military seized power in March 1976.

Nineteenth-century Traces
Buenos Aires' architectural history only really begins with its nineteenth-century expansion. A few small buildings remain from the

period of independence, including the oblong, yellow-painted Casa del Almirante Brown. William or Guillermo, (1777-1857) was an Irish-born naval man who migrated to Argentina and soon became the emerging nation's "first admiral", fighting against the Brazilians, the Spaniards and even the British. He lived in the "Yellow House" for more than 35 years following his retirement from active service, but it is in fact a replica which stands on the land he owned near Parque Lezama, close to the spot where Pedro de Mendoza first landed.

Almirante Brown often rode out from his house along the River Riachuelo, past the tanning factories where thousands of hides were cured and stored for export. Now the riverside area known as La Boca, where the original tin and wooden shacks have often been painted bright orange or green, is one of the city's main tourist attractions. But by far the most famous landmark not far from the admiral's house is the giant—and not nineteenth-century—football stadium officially known as the Estadio Alberto J. Armando, but universally called by its nickname La Bombonera, or "Box of Sweets". This is more because of its round shape than because of the warm welcome its gives to opposition fans, as this is the home of the Club Atlético Boca Juniors (Boca for short), which has one of the most ardent groups of *hinchas* or supporters in Argentina, if not the world.

It is said that the Boca teams owe their blue and yellow colours to the moment that in 1905 one of the club's five Italian founders saw a Swedish ship coming into dock nearby and, impressed with the strong colours of the national flag on the stern, adopted them for the newly-founded club. The current stadium was inaugurated on Independence Day in 1940, and can hold up to 57,000 people. The classic derby game in Argentine football pits Boca against River Plate, regarded by the Boca fans as snobs because that club's stadium is in the more middle-class northern neighbourhood of Nuñez (Belgrano). When the almost entirely open-air stadium is full for one of these games, the whole concrete bowl shakes alarmingly under the crowd's feet, while all kinds of missiles, from firecrackers to bricks, are exchanged between the opposing groups of supporters. For many years, Boca's most renowned player was Diego Armando Maradona (although his playing career began at another Buenos

Aires club, Argentina Juniors, whose stadium is now named after him). It was Maradona who asserted that this ground was "the temple of world football", and he is still a revered figure there and throughout Argentina. Since those glory days, however, the Boca club and Argentine football in general have fallen on harder times. Many of the country's best players (like Maradona in his day and Lionel Messi now) go abroad to earn more money, and the grounds themselves have suffered from a lack of investment due to the turbulent economic times that Buenos Aires and Argentina have been through in recent years. The football myth, though, survives as strongly as ever.

As the port of Buenos Aires grew in the second half of the nineteenth century, the need for transportation facilities and railways in particular became increasingly urgent. Perhaps the foremost iconic landmark of that era is the Retiro railway station and the area surrounding it. In the seventeenth century the flat ground down by the river to the north of the colonial city became a park, called the Retiro after the royal gardens in Madrid. By the early years of the next century it was known as the site of the main market for the captive slaves brought from Africa on British ships. This practice was ended in 1739, and by 1801 Retiro had become the place for the city's main bullring, which seated as many as 12,000 aficionados as well as doubling as a training ground for the recruits to General San Martín's forces who set out to liberate Chile a few years later.

The newly independent and progressive Argentina banned bullfighting as early as 1822. From this period onwards Retiro increasingly became a hub for port activity and was thus an obvious place to put the terminus for the burgeoning rail network to the cities further up the Río de la Plata (Rosario and Santa Fe) but also Córdoba, Tucumán and the other cities of the north such as Salta which had been so important as stopping-off points for the colonial trade through Peru, and now sent produce such as sugar, oranges, rice and minerals down to Buenos Aires. By the first decade of the twentieth century, the Argentine government wanted a new railway station that would reflect the country's booming economy and prominence in the world. The current Retiro station, likened to "a cathedral of the modern age", was designed by British architects and engineers. Its steel pillars and arches and the glass roof were built in Liverpool, transported by sea to Buenos Aires and re-assembled on site. As in Britain, the trains from Retiro served both long-distance destinations and the city suburbs (including the impeccably Anglo-Argentine suburb of Hurlingham), creating a commuter flow that is unique in Latin America.

As late as the 1980s, trains were leaving Retiro for the Bolivian border more than 3,000 kilometres (and two days and nights' ride) away, with dining cars still using heavy Sheffield plate cutlery and kitchenware. But the economic chaos of that decade led to huge underinvestment in the railway system, and a decade later the Carlos Menem government, which despite being Peronist in name was savagely neo-liberal in its economic policies, shut down many rail lines and privatized the more profitable ones. This marked the end of Retiro as one of the great centres of movement and life in Buenos Aires, as well as spelling decline for many communities in the north of the country which relied on the rail link to the capital. Perhaps inevitably, as Retiro was being made redundant as an invaluable railway terminus, in 1997 it was given the status of a national monument.

A sad coda to the vandalism of the Menem era was the fact that for many years almost the only trains coming and going from Retiro were transporting *cartoneros*. Particularly after the 2001 economic crash, the *cartoneros* were the poor from the provincial suburbs outside the capital who came into the city centre after dark to scavenge for cardboard boxes (*cartones*) and any other leftovers they could find in the streets that could be resold to make a few pence. Recently, however, some life has returned to Retiro station, as several of the long-distance trains have been re-established by private companies. There is even talk of a Japanese-style "bullet train" between Buenos Aires and Córdoba, but like many such grandiose schemes, this is likely never to come to fruition.

The square outside Retiro station also houses the main long-distance bus terminus, but in common with most bus stations throughout the world, this is dirty, smelly and architecturally undistinguished.

The bus and rail links with Argentina's poorer northern provinces, as well as Bolivia and Paraguay further north, also made Retiro a place where migrant workers congregated. From the 1930s on, the area between the station and the port was filled with thousands of shacks, often lacking any basic services. Successive governments promised to clear these *villas miseria* and re-house their inhabitants, but today Villa 31, a massive shanty town, still contains up to 30,000 people who have so far resisted all attempts to remove them. Another kind of memorial to the city's shifting population is not far from here: the famous (or infamous) Hotel de Inmigrantes (the Argentine equivalent of New York's Ellis Island), built in the early years of the twentieth century. It was here that the thousands of European immigrants flocking to Argentina were housed for five days after disembarkation, given health checks, and offered employment. The hotel ceased to function after 1953, but nowadays has been turned into the National Museum of Immigration.

In the centre of Retiro square stands another monument whose very name reflects the turbulent recent history of Argentina. This is what was known as the Torre de los Ingleses (the English Tower), so called because it was donated by the Anglo-Argentine community to celebrate the centenary of Argentina's independence from Spain in 1910. A red-brick tower in Palladian style, its height and its very English-looking clock made it a universally recognized emblem of the city. Because of the tower, the square itself was known as the Plaza Británica: that is, until 1982 and the war in the South Atlantic over the Malvinas/Falklands Islands. Following Argentina's defeat in that short-lived conflict, the tower was officially renamed the Torre de la Fuerza Aerea (Tower of the Air Force—because the Argentine pilots were those considered to have fought most bravely in the skies over the island). When patriotic passions died down in the 1990s the tower was again re-baptized the Torre Monumental; by now most *porteños* have reverted to calling it by its traditional name. A monument has now been erected facing the tower, at the foot of Parque San Martín. This is the wall containing 29 black marble plaques on which are inscribed the names of the 649 Argentine personnel killed in the 1982 war.

Above the memorial itself is Parque San Martín, which rises some thirty metres to the original level of the bluff above the river. It was the fresher air of this part of the city which led many of the wealthiest families to move here from the colonial centre around Plaza de Mayo, especially following the disastrous outbreak of yellow fever in 1871 which claimed more than 14,000 victims (almost eight per cent of the total population at the time). These families built huge mansions which they called *palacios* or palaces. Possibly the most famous and sumptuous of these was that lived in by the Anchorena family close to Parque San Martín on Calle Arenales. The Anchorena family came to the Río de la Plata region in the second half of the eighteenth century. The first generations were merchants, but by a hundred years later they were one of the largest landowners in Argentina. They were so fabulously rich that they are even mentioned in Argentina's great folk poem, *Martín Fierro*. Unlike many other landowning families, the Anchorenas successfully passed down this wealth through various generations. Possibly, as sociologist Juan José Sebreli points out, this is because they never sought political power in addition to their economic pre-eminence, although as he says: "together with another fifty families with whom they were linked by matrimony, friendship, or mutual interests, they made up the class which effectively ruled the country behind the puppet governments that formally did so."

Like many of their upper-class contemporaries, the Anchorenas moved from the south of the city near Plaza de Mayo to the northern area in the second half of the nineteenth century. Over the next fifty years they used their riches to build the largest private residences in the city. When one part of the family built the Palacio Ortiz Basualdo Anchorena close to Parque San Martín, the matriarch Doña Mercedes Castellanos de Anchorena decided she was not to be outdone, and so had her own, even larger mansion created almost opposite. This palace was built between 1905 and 1912 in the heavy French "belle époque" style then fashionable in Argentina (even though the architect Alejandro Christophersen was Norwegian by origin). The palace was the physical demonstration of the family's wealth, power and social position; as with many of the other ostentatious buildings in the Argentine capital, much of the stone and decorations were imported from Europe. Although from the outside the mansion looks to be one single building, with an elegant portico linking two heavy "Louvre" Second Empire-style blocks, it was built as three separate wings (with different layouts) joined by a central courtyard. Each wing was occupied by one of Doña Mercedes Castellanos de Anchorena's three sons and their families. The slated roofs with mansards and *oeil de boeuf* windows gave the mansion the french look so coveted by the Argentine upper class, and for two decades it was one of the centres of the city's social life. In 1928 the family between them still owned almost 400,000 hectares of land, mostly in Buenos Aires province, but the Great Depression, the division of properties and wealth among the new generations and the low profitability of land, meant that the Anchorena family was eventually forced to either sell or demolish their Buenos Aires palaces to make room for apartment buildings. The Plaza San Martín palace though was bought by the Argentine state. Since 1938 it has been occupied by the Foreign Ministry and renamed the Palacio San Martín, and its opulent salons, many with their original furnishings and decorations, are now used for state occasions.

The burgeoning nineteenth-century city also required another kind of palace: the most noteworthy of these tributes to progress and modernity is undoubtedly the Palacio de Aguas Corrientes (Central Pumping Station) built between 1887-94 at the highest point of the city on Avenida Córdoba to supply clean public drinking water. Occupying an entire block, its style is often described as "eclectic", meaning a conglomeration of European styles designed to impress by their weight and seriousness of intent. In common with most of the city's infrastructure of the period, the water supply was run by an English company, and the civil engineer John Bateman was put in charge of the building project. Bateman employed the Swedish architect Carlos Nystönner and the Dane Olof Boye to provide a suitably grand creation for this ambitious public works scheme, and the "palace" soon became one of Buenos Aires' most endearing landmarks. Its grandeur largely stems from the façade of the building, which is festooned with 170,000 ceramic tiles imported from Belgium and England, including thousands of polychrome terracotta pieces specially made by the Royal Doulton factories in the Potteries. The dark-green roof slates were also imported, this time from France. The interior is nowhere near as grand: the extravagant façade was built simply to house and hide four giant water tanks.

Palace of Culture

A very different kind of building that reflects the confidence and ambition of Buenos Aires as the centre of the country's cultural life is the Teatro Colón, a world-famous opera house. *Porteño* opera-goers (of whom there are many, perhaps thanks to the number of Italian, German and Jewish immigrants) like to compare the Colón's acoustics favourably with Milan's La Scala or the opera in Paris. The first Teatro Colón was constructed on Plaza de Mayo, but like many other institutions was transferred north at the end of the nineteenth century, and now stands facing the broad Avenida 9 de Julio.

It took from 1888 to 1908 to complete the new opera house, which was inaugurated on 25 May that year with a performance of Verdi's equally spectacular *Aïda*. The façade of the building is Greek revival in structure, whereas other parts have been described by one of the architects, Vittorio Meano, as possessing "the general characteristics of the Italian Renaissance, the careful distribution and solidity of German architecture, and the grace, variety and ornamental curiosity associated with French styles". In other words, the building offers the typical fusion (or collision) of an eclectic mixture of European architectural ideas of the time. The Teatro Colón is reputed to be the largest in such construction in the world, and can hold almost 2,500 seated spectators on seven levels, with a further 1,500 people standing in a traditional Italian horseshoe-shaped auditorium. The year 1925 saw the creation of the Colón's first stable orchestra, choir and ballet company, and these have been in existence ever since.

The fortunes of the Teatro Colón have closely followed those of Argentina as a whole. It took two decades for the building to be completed because of a financial crisis in the 1890s, and there have been similar ups and downs in its history throughout the twentieth century. In the 1920s Argentina was wealthy enough to be able to bring the greatest international opera and orchestral stars to perform in Buenos Aires (from Caruso to Richard Strauss). Even though the audiences were largely made up of Argentina's elite, such was the Colón's reputation for excellence that in the 1920s and 1930s it became common for crowds to shout at football or boxing matches *Al Colón! Al Colón!* whenever one of the sportsmen performed particularly brilliantly.

As a consequence of the economic crisis at the end of the 1920s, the opera house was taken over by the city authorities, who promoted local talent as well as visits from international figures. During the 1940s, Peronism was never kind to elite culture of the sort promoted by the Colón, and so during Perón's presidencies and the political upheavals surrounding them the theatre struggled to keep up its standards. It was then partially closed in 1988 because the hyperinflation afflicting Argentina made all future planning more or less impossible, and a similar situation led to a further crisis at the end of the 1990s. The return of a more stable economic situation after 2002 brought a fresh upturn in the opera house's fortunes, and in 2006 the authorities decided on a major overhaul and renovation of its facilities. These were completed in time for the Teatro Colón to stage a grand re-opening night for the 200th anniversary of Argentina's independence on 25 May 2010, although the event was marred because of a political spat between the Peronist President Cristina Fernández de Kirchner and the elected Mayor of Buenos Aires, the right-wing Mauricio Macri, which meant that the president refused to attend the grand re-opening event in a place run by the city authorities.

It was buildings such as the Teatro Colón which led Le Corbusier to describe Buenos Aires as the "centre of an imaginary empire"; but the place that epitomizes the most outlandish flights of this imagination is undoubtedly the Palacio Barolo, situated halfway along the Avenida de Mayo (no. 1370) between Plaza de Mayo and the disappointing Congreso building. This was the 1920s brainchild of a rich Italian immigrant, Luis Barolo, who had made his fortune producing cashmere sweaters. He contracted the Italian architect Mario Planti to build a physical representation of Dante's *Inferno:* it comprises three distinct levels (Hell, Purgatory and Heaven) plus a lighthouse on the top representing "the Empyrean". It measures a hundred metres in height—the number of cantos in *La Divina Comedia*—while its 22 floors represent the number of strophes in each canto. Barolo even attempted to buy Dante's tomb in Italy so that he could transport the great poet's remains to be placed in the basement of his building. Its style is unlike anything else in the city, with elements of Gothic and Islamic art in addition to mock Italian Renaissance features. The lighthouse on the roof was meant to communicate all the way across the Río de la Plata to the Palacio Salvo, an equally extravagant copy of the Buenos Aires building in the central square of the Uruguayan capital, Montevideo. Out of action for many decades, it was restored in recent years, and is now switched on once a month. In *Seconds Out*, a 2006 novel by the Argentine author Martín Kohan, the Palacio Barolo—"it is beautiful and horrible at the same time; it is sinister and endearing"—and its lighthouse play a crucial role. It is the colour of the light from the top that will tell the expectant crowds below whether or not the Argentine heavyweight boxing champion Luis Angel Firpo, known as the Wild Bull of the Pampas, has won the world title by defeating reigning champion Jack Dempsey. Without spoiling the plot of the novel, suffice it to say that Firpo knocks Dempsey out of the ring for seventeen seconds (*see www.youtube.com*) which means that the Barolo lighthouse proclaims Firpo's victory, only for the referee to rob him of his moment of glory. This miscarriage of justice was an early example that confirmed the *porteños'* belief that the rest of the world is against them, because they have the temerity to take on everyone else and be the best.

For more than a decade, the Palacio Barolo was the tallest building in downtown Buenos Aires. By the mid-1930s, however, more rational, modernist styles were making their impact, and the Kavanagh Building next to Parque San Martín (at Florida 1065), completed in 1936, is some twenty metres taller than the Italian extravaganza. At the time it was built, the Kavanagh was also the highest reinforced concrete structure in the world. What the Italian architect Mario Pelli has called "the only real skyscraper in Buenos Aires", and compared to the Chrysler Building in New York, is reputed to have been born out of a desire for revenge. Corina Kavanagh, a wealthy heiress of Irish descent, was said to have been so offended when the Anchorena family (see above) refused to allow one of their patrician sons to marry her daughter that she sold all her properties in order to build her own skyscraper which would not only dwarf their palace on the other side of Parque San Martín, but block the view of the Church of the Holy Sacrament that they had constructed as a private chapel nearby. Designed and built by local architects, it is a stunning combination of Art Deco and Modernism, with elegant lines, a lack of extraneous decoration that makes it the opposite of the Barolo, and 105 spacious apartments, the highest of which have superb roof gardens. Doña Kavanagh herself lived for many years on the fourteenth floor, able literally to look down on her snobbish neighbours.

The second half of the 1920s and the 1930s saw the construction of many other notable international modernist-style buildings. These included new factories along the newly-constructed Avenida General Paz, civic buildings and private residences. Possibly the most outstanding of these is the house which the rich patron of the arts Victoria Ocampo had built in 1928 in the upper-class residential district of Barrio Parque in the northern neighbourhood of Palermo (at Calle Rufino de Elizalde 2831). An Argentine architect, Alejandro Bustillo, was responsible for the white cube design of the exterior, while Ocampo herself helped plan the wide open spaces of the interior, which Le Corbusier himself described as being "of a purity I have rarely found". Built as it was in the midst of an area with many French-style mansions, the Ocampo house aroused a great deal of controversy due to its daring simplicity and functional design, which other local residents saw as spoiling the character of the neighbourhood. It was here that Ocampo founded *Sur*, the most important cultural magazine in Argentina in the 1930s and 1940s, and international writers and musicians such as

Bernard Shaw, Virginia Woolf, Igor Stravinsky and Maurice Ravel stayed here when they visited Buenos Aires.

Changing Cityscape

Argentina's distance from the great conflicts of the twentieth centuries means that it displays an unbroken continuity of building styles. There are proud civic buildings such as the Hospital de Clínicas and the University of Buenos Aires' Faculty of Medicine from the early 1940s, or the neo-fascist Faculty of Law built under Perón at the end of the same decade. Most of the construction in the city since then has been by private developers, who have built more and more high-rise apartment blocks, seemingly without any control by the city planning authorities. The Argentine novelist Julio Cortázar commented on how the city had changed since his childhood days in the 1930s:

> ... for a long time, Buenos Aires offered a horizontal view, the re-assuring proximity of walls and windows. Life in those days meant walking towards your neighbour, to go and meet others at the level of the tram-lines or the first floor. Nowadays it is all vertical skyscrapers, the river has disappeared, and in exchange we have innumerable cars lined up like a row of shoes.

Political and economic instability over the past sixty years has also contributed to this lack of significant contemporary architecture. For many years, planning for the future was risky, if not impossible. The cost and value of property swung widely depending on hyperinflation, dollarization and levels of employment. The Peronist government from 1947 to 1955 created the first cheap high-rise housing estates, mostly on the outskirts of the city, but few of these were architecturally distinguished. The military regimes, especially those from 1976 to 1983, were keener to build highways and other prominent infrastructure projects, although these also were often poorly constructed and in some cases left unfinished. It was not until Carlos Menem became president in 1989 and Argentina stabilized (for a while at least) both politically and financially, that interesting new projects began to flourish. Many of these were the kind of shopping mall to be found in any contemporary city. Others were luxury apartments in skyscrapers usually built to maximize profit. But the development of Puerto Madero, which took the city back out towards the river, not only managed to find a fresh use for the nineteenth-century brick warehousing and other port facilities, but brought international architects and designers to create striking new buildings. Among these are the Faena Hotel and Universe, a collaboration between the Argentine fashion designer Alan Faena and the French architect Philippe Starck, and the massive new museum housing the art collection of one of Argentina's wealthiest women, Amalia Lacroze de Fortabat.

Possibly the most iconic of these new architectural creations is the Puente de la Mujer (Woman's Bridge) that spans one of the old docks and was designed by the renowned Spanish architect Santiago Calatrava. Completed in 2001 (just before another economic crash) it is an asymmetrical cantilever bridge that can also swing through ninety degrees to allow boats to pass to the new marina. It is a pedestrian bridge some 170 metres long, and although some of the more exuberant tourist guides to Buenos Aires claim that the shape is symbolic of a couple dancing tango (the woman the horizontal shape, the vertical the man) it is the bridge's clear abstract lines that give it beauty.

As with every great city, the face of Buenos Aires is constantly changing. Its architecture reflects not only the lives of successive generations of its millions of inhabitants, but also provides a vivid metaphor for the unpredictable fortunes of the entire Argentine nation.

4

Rulers and Ruled
A Brief Social and Political History

When Juan de Garay sailed down the Río de la Plata in 1580, he had authorization as captain general from the Spanish emperor to found new settlements in the name of Spain. Although de Garay was the administrative head of the town, Buenos Aires and the other cities to the north in Argentina were accountable to the viceroy in Peru, who governed a vast territory stretching down from today's Ecuador as far as Chile. Buenos Aires was the empire's key port on the Atlantic seaboard, but the Spanish crown did not grant it the right to trade freely with other European nations. This meant that whatever was produced in the city or the surrounding pampas had to make a journey of several months north to the vice-regal port at Callao in Peru. It also meant that there was considerable temptation for the new settlement to deal in contraband goods.

Another tension that quickly emerged in the new settlement was the struggle for power between those born in Spain, and those who were second- or third-generation Americans. In 1617 Hernando Arias de Saavedra became the first of this latter group of *criollos* to head the government of Buenos Aires. Realizing that the spheres of influence of that city and Asunción de Paraguay were radically different, he petitioned the Spanish crown for their administrative separation. In 1617 a royal decree established Buenos Aires as the capital of the Río de la Plata region, making it no longer dependent on Asunción. Even so, the slowly growing port was still expressly forbidden to trade independently with the outside world, and in 1622 a customs post was set up on the road north at Córdoba, intended to protect the merchants of Peru against competition from the Buenos Aires traders. Despite these measures, contraband soon became one of the main driving forces behind the growth of the city, and led to the emergence of a trading class. A small bureaucratic elite also formed part of the colonial society, while beyond the limits

A soldier weeps at the funeral of Perón, July 1974
(Fernandopascullo/Wikimedia Commons)

of the city the first large landowners began to create and settle large estates for cattle and horse-rearing.

For several centuries, Buenos Aires was the southernmost outpost of the Spanish possessions to the east of the Andes. The indigenous peoples to the south fiercely resisted colonial expansion, and represented a sporadic threat to the city itself. It was not until the late nineteenth century that the territory to the west and south of Buenos Aires was forcibly cleared of the nomadic tribes, and Patagonia was settled by Europeans.

There were two other threats to the growth of Buenos Aires. The first of these was the Portuguese. From their bases in Brazil, Portuguese ships attacked the towns along the Río de la Plata. In 1726 the governor of Buenos Aires, Bruno de Zabala, founded the city of Montevideo on the eastern bank of the river to act as a bulwark against these incursions. Attempts to defend the Spanish possessions led to reinforcements in the military garrison at Buenos

Aires, creating another influential element among the population of the city.

The other centre of power in the newly-emerging colony was the Roman Catholic Church. Tensions between the Church and the temporal power fluctuated, mainly over the treatment of the indigenous population. They came to a head in the second half of the seventeenth century with the expulsion of the Jesuits from the whole of the Spanish empire. This was ordered in 1766 by Charles III, who saw the priests as a threat to imperial authority.

Ten years later another hugely significant step in the movement towards the independence of Buenos Aires and Argentina as a whole occurred. A Spanish royal decree dated 19 August 1776 established the viceroyalty of the Río de la Plata. As a result, Buenos Aires was no longer subject to the authorities in Peru, and the new administrators controlled a vast territory that included Paraguay and the fabulously rich city of Potosí in Bolivia as well as Salta, Tucumán and other towns in the north-west of what was to become the Argentine nation. The first viceroy of this autonomous region was Pedro de Cevallos. In 1777 he brought in legislation allowing Buenos Aires to trade freely with Peru and Chile, followed shortly afterwards by the legalization of trade between the port and the mother country, Spain. These measures brought fresh vigour to the city, and helped make it the centre for products from the towns of the interior, which could be much more easily exported from Buenos Aires than via the Pacific Coast. Public finances were boosted soon afterwards, when a customs post was set up in the city. Trade was given a further impetus in 1791, when a decree permitted the foreign ships bringing slaves and manufactures to Argentina to take local products directly back to their home countries. Cevallos' successor Juan José de Vértiz y Salcedo was another promoter of free trade and progressive Enlightenment values.

Towards Independence

By the last decade of the eighteenth century, Spain was losing control of its vast overseas empire. The riches that had poured back to the peninsula had largely been wasted on wars and poor administration, while the control exercised on thought by the Spanish Inquisition and other reactionary forces within the Church and Spanish society had rendered Spain increasingly inward-looking and left behind by countries such as Britain, Holland and France. Not only were these nations embarking on agricultural and industrial revolutions, but fresh ideas and political ideologies were emerging, whereas Spain was still stuck in its quasi-medieval past. In 1789 the French Revolution brought this conflict between the old and new political and economic worlds to crisis point. Manuel Belgrano, who became head of the Buenos Aires Consulate, a powerful local government institution set up around this time, vigorously championed the ideals of free trade and liberalism.

The French Revolution soon gave way to Napoleon and his own attempts to build an empire. The British were at war with France, but also saw the opportunity to move against Spain's colonial possessions in South America. In June 1806 a fleet under the command of General Beresford appeared off Buenos Aires. His men occupied the fort in the centre of the city. Some of the merchants welcomed this English invasion, but Santiago de Liniers (1753-1810) crossed to Montevideo and organized an army there. Returning to Buenos Aires in August, his troops besieged the fortress, and Beresford capitulated a few days later.

This successful resistance had further political repercussions in the city. The Spanish-appointed viceroy, Rafael de Sobremonte, had fled when the British fleet appeared, and in February 1807 Liniers and an open council or *cabildo abierto* ruled that he should be deposed and that the members of the Royal Audience should take over his role. This new administration was soon put to the test: in June of that same year, another British force, led this time by John Whitelocke, again made an invasion attempt. Once again Liniers and the militia he had organized (including the Patricios regiment, which still guards the presidential palace today) succeeded, with the help of many of the inhabitants of Buenos Aires, in compelling the invaders to surrender. Although largely unknown in Britain, these two invasion attempts and their successful repulsion loom large in the history of Buenos Aires and Argentina. On the one hand, they are seen as proof of the rapacious nature of "imperialism"; on the other, they are seen as proof of the fighting qualities and determination of Argentines when they unite in a just cause.

In 1810 Napoleon's forces took over Spain. His brother Joseph was installed as king, and the centuries-old Spanish empire was on the point of collapse. When this news reached Buenos Aires, there were immediate calls for the new viceroy Cisneros to step down. At the end of May 1810 another open council was called. The viceroy and his supporters argued that nothing should change, but the *criollos* demanded that Cisneros be replaced by a junta chosen by the inhabitants of the port. At first the Spanish appointees would not agree, but pressure from the streets on 25 May 1810 led to the creation of a "popular junta" of the leading *criollo* politicians and intellectuals. Argentina dates its independence from this day, but in fact this was only the start of the struggle to free Buenos Aires and the rest of the country from Spanish domination.

Many of the cities in the interior were opposed to radical change, as it was likely to undermine their economic position. The new junta had to send military expeditions to Córdoba, where they defeated a loyalist army, and to Paraguay, where the junta's forces were defeated. In Buenos Aires, the struggle continued between representatives of the provinces and those of the capital, headed by Mariano Moreno, who sought to impose liberal, free-trade views on the rest of the country. Moreno established a triumvirate, rejected the demands of the provincial capitals for representation, and prepared to do battle with them and all those who wished Buenos Aires to remain loyal to Spain.

Despite initial successes, in October 1812 the triumvirate was toppled by a military clique led by José de San Martín. The victors convened a constituent assembly, which at the end of January 1813 declared the independence of Argentina, with a new national anthem and the flag of blue-and-white stripes with a central golden sun that is still in use today. All titles of nobility were abolished, and children born of slaves were declared to be free citizens. But the divisions between those like Carlos María de Alvear (named "Supreme Director" in January 1815), who saw Buenos Aires as the powerful capital of a unified country, and those who wanted a more federal system, undermined the strength of the emerging nation.

A congress was called in the city of Tucumán to draw up a national constitution. Independence from Spain was declared once more, on 9 July 1816 (hence the Avenida 9 de Julio named many years later). Yet the struggle between the provinces and Buenos Aires only worsened, until in 1820 the provincial forces defeated those of the Directorate supporting Buenos Aires. Subsequently, a new constitution based on independent provinces (with Buenos Aires one among many) was signed. In spite of the failure of its attempts at hegemony within the new nation, the years from 1820 to 1824 saw Buenos Aires grow rapidly, thanks mainly to the leadership of Bernardino Rivadavia. Under his rule, the Catholic Church lost many of its privileges, primary schools sprang up throughout the city, the Colegio de la Unión offered enlightened secondary education to boys, and the University of Buenos Aires was founded on 12 August 1821. More than ever, Buenos Aires was the vital link between the rich interior provinces and the outside world. When in 1824 Spain renounced its claim on its former South American possessions, several countries including Britain, France and the United States set up consulates in the city. A stock exchange was established, and Baring Brothers, the bank established in London for several hundred years (until it was bankrupted by a "rogue trader" in the 1990s) lent the government of Buenos Aires one million pounds sterling—the start of a history of indebtedness to foreign institutions that left-wing commentators in Argentina have frequently deplored. Eduardo Galeano for example, in *The Open Veins of Latin America*, claims that the debt was not repaid until the start of the twentieth century, by which time it had mushroomed to £4 million. But this loan was used by Rivadavia not only to bring in better breeds of cattle and sheep for the pampas, but to set up scientific and other educational centres, as well as on many improvements to the city.

The following years saw wars against Brazil, when Almirante Brown (see p. 41) became a national hero by defeating the larger Brazilian fleet on several occasions, and continuing civil strife as the provinces along the river, the interior, and Buenos Aires fought for supremacy. As president of the United Provinces of the Río de la Plata in 1826-27, Rivadavia was accused of weakness when he allowed the eastern bank of the river—the Banda Oriental—to break away and form the independent state of Uruguay. He was eventually toppled, and there followed several more years of uncertainty, until the first of a long line of Argentine *caudillos* or strong men took charge.

Dictators and Civil War

This man was Juan Manuel de Rosas. Elected as governor of Buenos Aires province for five years in 1829, he was only finally forced from office 23 years later in 1852. He ruled what was known as the Federation of Provinces continuously from 1835, when a free vote of all male inhabitants of Buenos Aires resulted in him being overwhelmingly elected as president for life. Known as the "Restorer of the Laws", Rosas took the city and country back to an almost colonial structure, with rule centralized in Buenos Aires, the Catholic Church once more given the leading role in education, and the position of the big landowners further strengthened. He also began the "wars of the desert", military campaigns which saw the indigenous groups pushed further and further south into Patagonia. The conquered land was not offered to new farmers, but shared out among Rosas' followers and already established landowners. This kept the provinces backward-looking, still relying on exports of hides and salted meat and dependent on a few powerful local figures.

Rosas has long been a controversial figure in Argentine history. He portrayed himself as the strong leader the country needed in order to keep division and anarchy at bay. Charles Darwin, who visited him in 1833, considered him to be "a most predominant influence in the country, which it seems he will use to its prosperity and advancement". Others have seen him in a much more negative light, pointing to his creation of a police state in which opposition was put down by his fanatical supporters, who were banded together in a paramilitary group known as *La Mazorca* (the Corn Cob). No dissent was tolerated. Prominent writers and intellectuals such as

Juan Alberdi and Domingo Faustino Sarmiento (both of them later to become presidents) were among the first of many generations of Argentine dissidents forced into exile. (The 1984 film *Camila* by María Luisa Bemberg memorably recreates the atmosphere of persecution that reigned in those days.)

By the early 1850s Rosas faced increasing unrest from provincial governors and from Uruguay. The most powerful of these opponents was the governor of Entre Ríos, Justo José de Urquiza. At the end of 1851 Urquiza assembled a large army which marched on Buenos Aires. Rosas and his federal forces were routed at the Battle of Caseros. The "Restorer of the Laws" was forced into exile and lived out the rest of his life near Southampton in England, where he died in 1877. Buried in the local cemetery there, his remains were finally returned to Argentina in 1989 as a gesture of goodwill as part of the restoration of relations between the United Kingdom and Argentina following the 1982 Malvinas/Falklands War. His tomb is now in La Recoleta cemetery in the centre of Buenos Aires.

Urquiza set about trying to unite the country with the promulgation of a new constitution. Based on that of the United States, the new Argentine charter proposed a representative republican democracy with a strong executive. Individual rights were enshrined in it, as was the federal nature of the republic; the 1853 constitution also included clauses aimed at distributing wealth—concentrated to a large extent in Buenos Aires province—throughout the rest of the new nation. These measures led the government of Buenos Aires to reject the new constitution, which was passed by all the other provinces on 9 July 1853. The split between the two sides was made complete in April 1854 when the State of Buenos Aires passed its own fundamental charter. Urquiza was elected president of the interior provinces, and ruled from Paraná, while in Buenos Aires Valentín Alsina soon became governor. It was not long before an economic battle broke out, with each taxing goods from the other. Eventually the conflict led to open warfare. Urquiza once more led an army against the forces from Buenos Aires, commanded by General Bartolomé Mitre. On 23 October 1859 General Urquiza's

Confederate forces won a victory at the Battle of Cepeda, and Urquiza set up his headquarters in the Buenos Aires neighbourhood of San Juan de Flores.

Both sides, however, seemed willing to reach a compromise, and in November 1859 the treaty of union between Buenos Aires and the Confederation was signed. Buenos Aires accepted the 1853 constitution and agreed to be part of a unified nation, while the revenues from the Buenos Aires customs taxes were allotted to the entire country. The pact did not last long. By 1861 the two sides were fighting once more: this time Urquiza was defeated by Mitre at the Battle of Pavón. Nominated as president, Mitre overturned the 1853 constitution, made Buenos Aires the national capital, and dissolved the Confederation. In many ways, the year 1862 can be seen as the start of modern-day Argentina, with Buenos Aires as its all-powerful capital.

President Mitre and the two men who followed him in office (Domingo Faustino Sarmiento from 1868 to 1874 and Nicolás Avellaneda from 1874 to 1880) set about laying the foundations of the modern state. The problems of the relationship between Buenos Aires and the national government, and central control over the provinces, were tackled vigorously. The provincial armies were merged into a national force. Federal systems of justice and taxation were also created. However, the precise role of the city of Buenos Aires within the nation still created conflict. This was not finally resolved until 1880, when a law passed by the national Congress named Buenos Aires as the federal capital of the republic, separating it from Buenos Aires province. By then, mass immigration and economic growth had begun to change the face of Buenos Aires forever.

Conflicting Interests

The period between 1880 and 1916 came to be known as the Liberal Republic. Argentina's agricultural exports to Europe made it one of the richest countries in the world. The introduction of ways to first freeze and then chill beef and mutton so that carcasses could be exported to Europe gave this export-dominated model a further boost. The port of Buenos Aires became lined with *frigoríficos*, where the slaughtered cattle were stored for shipment overseas. Like many areas of the export economy, the chilling facilities were owned by the British. Three centuries after its foundation, Buenos Aires was the increasingly powerful centre of an economic system based on agricultural exports produced by a small number of landowners, and the import of consumer goods for the middle classes, but also increasingly for the paid workforce attracted from the poorer regions of Europe. The system's apparent success acted as a brake on attempts to diversify the local economy and to produce goods in Argentina itself. However, by 1886 even the British newspaper *The Financial Times* was warning of its inherent dangers: "Apart from the corrupt politicians, the greatest enemy of a healthy Argentine currency has been the estancia owners. As the chief landowners and producers in the country, their interest lies in being able to pay their costs in paper money and gain high prices in gold for the sale of their products. Their idea of paradise is based on good markets in Europe and a poor currency in their own country, because in this way gold provides them with land and a cheap workforce."

In that same year, one of these landowners, Miguel Juárez Celman, the leader of the traditional Partido Autonomista Nacional or Nationalist Party, became president thanks to a fraudulent election. During his term in office he busily sold off public assets to line his and his friends' pockets. This created a boom on the nascent stock market in Buenos Aires, and for the private banks he had encouraged, until the end of 1889, when prices for Argentina's exports fell sharply in international markets. Throughout the next year the *bolsa* or stock exchange experienced a crash that was to become the first of several similar financial crises over the next century. This crash was graphically portrayed in one of the early works of Argentine fiction, *La Bolsa*, by Julián Martel (real name José María Miró), published in 1891. In Chapter Ten, Margarita, the wife of one of main characters, shows that she is well aware of what is going on: "she read in the newspapers the movement of the Stock Exchange. Something strange, inexplicable had taken place there. The Banks had suspended all credit, and were not lending a peso to anyone, absolutely no-one. Gold was still high, and balancing the books at the end of the month threatened to be a disaster. The names of important businesses that were seriously at risk were being whispered. As for individuals going bankrupt, especially brokers, there were said to be dozens of cases. Land values had suddenly fallen, and panic reigned everywhere."

By June 1890 the Celman government was forced to default on its foreign debt. Those with savings in the private Argentine banks scrambled to withdraw their money, so that many of them went bankrupt. Stocks fell dramatically on the *bolsa*, and soon many companies had to close, causing a huge rise in unemployment. In Europe, those who had invested in Argentina faced calamitous losses: the London-based Baring Brothers bank, which had made one of the first big loans to the government of the newly independent Argentina in the 1820s, threatened it would declare itself bankrupt unless its creditors paid up. There were even rumours that Germany might invade Argentina to recover its debts. In July 1890, the streets of Buenos Aires witnessed the kind of military uprising that was to become sadly familiar over the following decades. For three days there was a standoff between the rebel forces commanded by General Campos, drawn up in what nowadays is the Plaza Lavalle in the heart of the city, and troops loyal to the Celman government. In the end, bloodshed was avoided when President Celman stepped down. He was replaced by his vice-president, Carlos Pelligrini, who set about restoring stability thanks to a patriotic fund to help meet foreign debt requirements, the closure of most of the remaining private banks, and the establishment of the Banco de la Nación as the only entity authorized to issue currency. These measures were enough to help the recovery of Argentina and Buenos Aires as its commercial and political hub.

One positive outcome of the 1890 crisis was the weakening of the Partido Autonomista. A new political grouping that was to have a great impact on the political life of Argentina was created. This was the Unión Cívica (later to become the Radical Party). The year 1895 saw the creation of the Socialist Party under the leadership of Juan B. Justo. The traditional power elites began to face increasing challenges. Demands for greater political representation rose to the surface once more in 1902, when a general strike paralyzed Buenos Aires. President Roca responded by introducing the "law of residence", which empowered the authorities to deport any foreign born citizens suspected of "disturbing public order". Repression led to further demonstrations, which were aggressively broken up by the police and army. Despite these obstacles, the workers' movement continued to grow strongly: in 1904 Alfredo Palacios, was elected to Congress as the first Socialist Party representative. Increased political unrest in 1909 and 1910 led to electoral reforms which made voting (still restricted to men) secret and compulsory. Mass immigration and changes in Argentina's social structure meant that the conservatives in the Nationalist Party could no longer easily keep a stranglehold on power.

Many of the new immigrants, as well as the expanding middle classes of professionals and civil servants, were attracted to the new Radical Party and the man who was now its charismatic leader Hipólito Yrigoyen. In the 1916 elections, the Radical Party won victory for the first time, and Yrigoyen became president. The Radicals were to remain in power for the next fourteen years. At first they benefitted from the increased prosperity that the First World War brought for Argentina's food exports, but increasingly proved unable to cope with the divisions that the spectacular growth in population—much of it concentrated in Buenos Aires—created in the country. In 1919, what became known as the *semana trágica* or "tragic week", the government violently suppressed demonstrations by the Union of Metalworkers, who were calling for a reduction in working hours, Sundays without work and wage increases. Estimates of the numbers killed in that week vary between one and four hundred people; some 50,000 were arrested. In its attempts to justify the repression, the Radical government used slogans that were to be heard time and again throughout the following decades: the disturbances were caused by "anarchists", "provocateurs" or "foreign troublemakers". As usual, there was little acknowledgement of the claims the protestors were making.

At the same time, the traditional right-wing landowners and their allies in business and the armed forces grew increasingly opposed to the timid reforms introduced by the Radicals. While Argentina's economy was booming in the immediate post-war years, this opposition was muted. But in the second half of the 1920s the rise of fascism in Italy found an echo among these groups. When the world economy came crashing down in 1929, and the impact began to be felt in Argentina, the armed forces under General José F. Uriburu made their move. Hipólito Yrigoyen, by now old and out of touch with events, was toppled.

What followed came to be known as the "infamous decade". It also marked the start of a much longer period during which the Argentine armed forces played an overtly political role in the life of the nation. Throughout the 1930s there was massive fraud at each election to ensure that the right-wing forces stayed in power and continued to repress political and trade union opposition, particularly in the capital. Despite this, the working-class movement grew and became more influential, especially in the greater Buenos Aires area, where new industries had sprung up. By the end of the decade, more than a million Argentines were working in industry. The main trade union body representing them was the Confederación General de los Trabajadores (CGT), which was formed in 1937 and soon became the most powerful union grouping. Throughout the 1930s Buenos Aires and other industrial centres were in ferment. The right-wing politicians and the military resorted to terror to suppress all calls for social and political reform, but rapidly increasing numbers of workers as well as a radicalized lower middle class continued to put pressure on the rigid political system.

Perón and After

At the outbreak of the Second World War the government and the armed forces in Argentina were divided. While Argentina officially remained neutral, some in Ramón S. Castillo's government favoured the United States, while others, particularly in the military, were more in sympathy with the Axis powers. These tensions came to a head on 4 June 1943, when supporters of the latter view among a group of officers known as the GOU (Grupo de Oficiales Unidos) removed President Castillo in a bloodless coup. Despite their title, the officers now in power proved anything but united. This gave the opportunity to one of the young colonels, Juan Domingo Perón, to stake his claim. While serving in Italy for a year in 1938, he had been impressed by the way that Mussolini's fascist government controlled the mass union movement. Back in Argentina, as Labour Minister he cultivated links with the CGT and other unions, establishing a strong power base among them. Perón's rapid rise was soon seen as a threat by many of the other officers in government, and in October 1945 they demanded his resignation and threatened to put him on trial.

The popular response to this move has become a central part of the mythology of "Peronism" and of Buenos Aires. On 17 October 1945 thousands of his supporters, most of them workers from the new industrial suburbs, marched through the streets of Buenos Aires towards Plaza de Mayo, demanding that Perón be set free. The government eventually yielded to this pressure, and Perón made the first of his many appearances on the balcony of the Casa Rosada to harangue the huge crowd of his followers.

The military government also agreed that general elections could be held at the start of 1946, with Colonel Perón allowed to stand. The traditional political parties had little response to his new message aimed directly at the working class (who soon became known as the *descamisados*, the people who take off their shirts to do the hard work). Perón won a clear victory at the 24 February 1946 elections, and Peronism was born. At first the new president was supported by sectors of the armed forces and the Catholic Church as well as by the organized workers and many in the rural interior. His rule, though, was authoritarian from the start: he gave his supporters jobs throughout the public administration, from Supreme Court judges to university professors. As under Rosas, many intellectuals went into exile, including the writer Julio Cortázar. But Perón and his second wife Eva held decisive control over the masses. They were both experts in the use of radio and the other media to forge an emotional link with all those who felt that the traditional political parties in Argentina had left them on the margins. Thanks to Evita (the affectionate diminutive of her name), women were given the vote in 1947; other measures saw more workers gain paid holidays and social security benefits. Argentina was once again in a fortunate position after the Second World War, as Europe was desperate for its agricultural exports; Perón used the money to promote national industries and infrastructure. One of his most spectacular gestures was the purchase of the national railway network in 1947 from the British companies who had been running it until then, handing over what was reputed to be the largest cheque ever signed to that date.

Perón won a second term in office in 1951. But by now the tide was turning against him. Inflation eroded the gains the workers had made, and the traditional right wing, together with the armed forces began to withdraw their support. The death of Evita in 1952 led to mass mourning on the streets of Buenos Aires, but also marked a further decline in Perón's ability to keep the military and conservatives happy, in addition to the increasingly well-organized workers. The political right and the Catholic Church moved to open opposition when he tried to bring in laws allowing divorce and abortion. In June 1955 Perón was excommunicated; when he called for a mass rally of support on 26 June 1955, Argentine naval planes bombarded the demonstration in Plaza de Mayo in a direct attempt to kill the president. They failed in this, but did cause the deaths of 364 of their fellow countrymen and women. The Peronists responded by sacking several churches and the metropolitan cathedral, but by now the writing was on the wall. In September of the same year, a rebellion by the armed forces led to a coup that overthrew Perón and ushered in what was called the "Liberating Revolution".

For almost two decades thereafter, the armed forces attempted to rule Argentina either directly or through elections from which the Peronists were excluded. Peronist unions were prohibited, and many of the measures Perón had introduced were overturned. While the landowners and the middle classes in Buenos Aires could enjoy their newfound freedom, attempts to govern the country while excluding the majority of the population were doomed to failure. In 1958 Arturo Frondizi was elected thanks to a deal with former President Perón exiled in Madrid, who called on his supporters to back the Radical Party politician. Frondizi opened up the country's oil industry, and brought in foreign investment that saw new industries spring up on the outskirts of Buenos Aires and elsewhere in the country. But his hold on power, together with that of his two civilian successors, was tenuous, squeezed between the powerful trade unions that stayed loyal to the "old man" in Madrid, and the various factions in the armed forces. It was in the early 1960s that the streets of the capital began to witness random violence perpetrated by Peronists and their opponents, as well as the sight of army tanks sweeping into the city and fighting battles against other military units. The hapless civilian administrations were unable to control these far more powerful forces. Historian Eduardo Crawley describes the bloodless end of President Arturo Illia's rule on 28 June 1966:

> The Casa Rosada began to be occupied by the military, but still Illia did not budge from his office. Finally, a squad of the Guardia de Infanteria, the riot unit of the Federal Police, was ordered to dislodge the President, taking care to do him no personal harm. This they achieved by gently pushing the ring of young Radicals, who had protectively surrounded Illia, out of his office and into the street. Illia haughtily refused the offer of the presidential limousine to drive him home. Instead, he hailed a taxi and disappeared into the night.

This night was to last many years. The 1966 coup was grandiosely named the "Argentine Revolution". The new military president, Juan Carlos Onganía, dissolved Congress, the provincial legislatures and all political parties, and there was no promise to return to elected rule. In Buenos Aires the authorities bulldozed all the popular informal restaurants or *carritos* along the *costanera* riverfront—in the name of health and safety. Repression began against the universities: the premises of the University of Buenos Aires were stormed by the police, and hundreds of arrests made. This "night of the long batons" marked the start of a fresh exodus of academics and intellectuals that was to become a flood over the next twenty years. However, as with earlier military regimes, General Onganía had little to offer beyond repression. Popular opposition to his rule grew, and the Peronist unions were always a threat. A new danger was posed by the small guerrilla groups that sprang up, aiming to bring revolution to Argentina and beginning with bank robberies, kidnappings and bomb attacks that made the streets of Buenos Aires increasingly unsafe. By the early 1970s the military, now led by General Alejandro Lanusse, announced that elections would be held, and that the Peronists would be allowed to stand for the first time in eighteen years.

General elections were held in March 1973, with the Peronists allowed to participate. Hector Cámpora, the Peronist presidential candidate, won a comfortable victory, and this paved the way for the return of the man himself. On 20 June, almost two million Argentines from Buenos Aires and every corner of the country went out to Ezeiza airport to welcome Juan Domingo Perón back after more than seventeen years of forced exile. What should have been a moment of triumph and celebration turned into a bloodbath that was a foretaste of the years of violence to come. Shooting started between young left-wing supporters of Perón, many of them in the clandestine Montonero organization, and Perón's right-wing union security guards. Before the day was out, many people who had come to hail the return of their hero lay dead or wounded. Perón himself had an inglorious return to the small military airport at Morón.

In the months that followed, Campora stepped down, and *el gran lider* was elected president for a third time, at the age of 78. Any hopes that Perón's re-appearance would somehow magically cure the country's many ills were dashed with his death in July 1974. As with Evita, hundreds of thousands of people crowded the streets of Buenos Aires at his funeral. But his third wife, María Estela (known by the Peronist faithful as "Isabelita") was incapable of holding the different factions of the movement together. This had disastrous results. Inspired by the Argentine revolutionary "Che" Guevara and the success of the Cuban revolution, young people in Buenos Aires and elsewhere in the country came to believe they could overthrow the state by violent means and install a revolutionary left-wing government. These groups often used kidnappings and bombings to create a climate of insecurity in the capital: by 1975 a bomb was going off every few minutes. They were opposed at first by the police and paramilitary squads such as the Argentine Anti-Communist Alliance (AAA), who used illegal force to counteract the Montoneros, the People's Revolutionary Army (ERP) and other smaller revolutionary groups.

The armed forces were brought in by the Peronist administration to quash the rural guerrilla movement in the north of the country, while for many months Buenos Aires and the other big cities were gripped by violence as Isabelita's government foundered. In March 1976, after many months of rumours, a military junta formed by the three branches of the armed forces toppled Isabel Perón and seized power. The coup was initially welcomed by many sectors of Argentine society, who thought the military could restore order. In Buenos Aires, Congress was closed, trade unionists and Peronist activists were rounded up, and all political activity banned. At the same time, the armed forces began a campaign designed to get rid of what they termed "subversion" once and for all.

Military Rule

This period, which particularly affected life in the capital, later became known as the "dirty war", a term originally used by the junta to justify its use of illegal means to counter the perceived threat from left-wing guerrilla groups. The terror that followed the 1976 military takeover reached unprecedented levels. The security forces snatched anyone they thought might be involved in revolutionary or simply opposition activity, and "disappeared" them. This meant that somewhere between 9,000 and 30,000 Argentines simply vanished without trace: the authorities denied all knowledge of their whereabouts, no writs of *habeas corpus* were granted, and there was no admission of what was going on. In the southern winter of 1976 and throughout 1977 thousands of Argentines and scores of foreigners were seized, tortured and then killed by agents of the state, although it is now widely accepted that the would-be revolutionary groups had been roundly defeated much earlier. Grotesquely, this campaign was partly aimed at pacifying the capital and other cities before the June 1978 Football World

Cup, which Argentina duly won. Official buildings in Buenos Aires became clandestine torture centres. The most notorious of these was the Navy School of Mechanics (ESMA), where as many as 5,000 prisoners were tortured, killed and their bodies disposed of in secret (sometimes by taking the prisoners, still alive, in aircraft out over the Río de la Plata, then jettisoning them into the water). Other torture centres such as El Vesuvio, a clandestine army centre on the outskirts, remain as mute witnesses of the years of horror in the capital. The ESMA itself has been turned into a 'space for memory', where visitors are invited to reflect on the horrors committed by organs of the state in the years 1976–1983. Thousands more Argentines were forced into exile; most families knew of someone who had been "disappeared", although few people dared talk about the situation.

The military rulers also pursued economic policies that saw Peronist protectionism and state enterprises replaced by investment from abroad and private initiative. Peronist attempts to encourage radio and TV to promote national culture were replaced by a flood of foreign imports of music and films, while the juntas opened Buenos Aires and the country as a whole to the rest of the world. Most large firms, universities and even schools, had a military *interventor* who kept a close watch on their activities. The military authorities borrowed heavily to initiate large infrastructure projects such as the elevated highways lengthening Avenida 9 de Julio, many of which were not completed after the funds ran out. However, by start of the 1980s, the military's attempts to prolong their stay in power were running into difficulty. Their economic policies were producing inflation and unemployment, and the welcome they had enjoyed from many middle-class Argentines was exhausted. So it was that in April 1982 the most recent head of the junta, General Leopoldo Fortunato Galtieri, tried a desperate gamble. He sent Argentine forces to take over the Falkland Islands, which called the Islas Malvinas and had claimed as part of their national territory for many years despite their occupation by settlers from Britain since the 1830s. Caught unawares, the small British garrison was forced to surrender, and Argentine forces took control of the archipelago. For the first time since the military takeover in 1976, the Plaza de

Mayo was filled by huge crowds cheering on their armed forces and the military rulers.

Little more than two months later, what had been heralded as a *gesta* or noble military exploit had become a humiliating defeat. The Argentine army, made up largely of poorly trained and equipped conscripts, proved no match for British troops who had sailed eight thousand miles to retake the islands. After the Argentine surrender on 14 June 1982, *porteños* flocked into the streets once more, this time demanding that the military leaders step down. After a short transition period, elections were held in late 1983. Many voters still held the Peronists to blame for starting the violence that had brought unheard-of repression to the country, and so for the first time in many years a Radical Party government was elected under President Raúl Alfonsín. The new president made strenuous efforts to uncover everything that had taken place during the years of military rule and set up a commission to look into all the disappearances. Such was the mistrust of politicians or other public figures that he appointed the novelist Ernesto Sábato chairman of this body, known as the Commission on the Disappearance of Persons (CONADEP). Its report *Nunca Más* (Never Again) was published in 1985. It gave details of some 9,000 disappearances at the hands of state security forces, more than half of them from the capital or greater Buenos Aires. The Alfonsín government also brought the members of the different juntas to trial in Buenos Aires in April 1985. They were given sentences varying between life and seven years in military jail. Thanks to the *Nunca Más* report and the trials, more and more stories of horror surfaced. Argentines had to come to terms with the terror unleashed by the security forces in their name—and more than that, many of the torturers and people who had collaborated (from figures in authority in the Roman Catholic Church to doctors and policemen) were still in their posts. Elements within the army regarded these efforts by the civilian governments as betrayal, and President Alfonsín had to face three rebellions during his time in office. The most serious of these came in Easter Week 1987, when Plaza de Mayo filled with people once more, determined to defend their democratically elected government.

Fragile Democracy

Although pressure from the military was resisted, President Alfonsín was not so successful in economic affairs. By the end of the 1980s hyperinflation (which reached more than 2,000 per cent in some months) made daily life in Buenos Aires chaotic. As a result not only did the Radicals lose the 1989 elections, but Alfonsín was forced to leave office several months early because of the economic turmoil and hand over to the Peronist Carlos Menem. Although seen as a traditionalist figure within Peronism, Preisdent Menem immediately began to implement neoliberal policies that ran counter to what previous Peronist administrations had supported. Not only did he open the country to foreign investment but he sold off many state-run enterprises. The main plank in his economic programme, however, was to create parity between the Argentine peso and the US dollar, a move which brought much-needed stability and created a construction boom in the capital. Works that had been stalled for several years were begun again, and new buildings sprang up everywhere. Grandiose projects such as Puerto Madero (see p. 34) were undertaken along with new shopping malls, and there was a general transfer from public to private. The railways, which had suffered years of little or no investment, were closed down, the number of private cars on the capital's streets mushroomed, and *porteños* began to travel abroad once more.

In 1994, President Menem brought in constitutional changes, mainly to allow himself to stand for a second term as president, but also and more importantly for Buenos Aires, bringing in an elected mayor or *intendente*, with control over the budget of what was now termed "the autonomous city". As in other countries of Latin America such as Colombia or Chile, the elected mayor of the capital has often pursued different policies from the national government. The Radical Party's Fernando de la Rúa was the first elected mayor in 1996. He used his position as a stepping stone to stand for the presidential elections, which he won in 1999. He was followed as mayor of the city by the Socialist Aníbal Ibarra, who was also seen as a possible presidential candidate until at the end of 2004 a disastrous fire broke out in the República Cromañon nightclub, in which as many as 200 people perished. As a result, the Buenos Aires legislature voted to impeach Mayor Ibarra, and he was forced to step down in early 2006. Now in a second period in office, the mayor since 2007 has been Mauricio Macri, a prominent businessman who is also the chairman of La Boca football club. He has become the most prominent right-wing leader in Argentina, often opposing the policies of the Peronist governments led firstly by Néstor Kirchner, then by his wife and now widow Cristina Fernández de Kirchner.

The Peronists have been in power in the country for all but five years since the last military regime. Carlos Menem enjoyed two terms in office from 1989 to 1999, when he was replaced by the Radical Party's Fernando de la Rúa. Although this was seen as a sign of the maturity of Argentina's electorate, who responsibly voted for alternation in power, the Radical government once again ended in disarray. By the end of 2000 hyperinflation was back with a vengeance. Support for the president and his party plummeted. By December 2001 thousands of demonstrators took to the streets of Buenos Aires often chanting the slogan *Que se vayan todos!* ("Get rid of the lot of them!") These protests were again repressed by the police, leaving more than twenty people dead. Shortly before Christmas 2001 de la Rúa was ignominiously plucked out of the Casa Rosada in a helicopter. Over the next fortnight, Argentina had three presidents as they grappled to bring the social and economic chaos under control. The following months saw the Argentine peso devalued. The government refused to pay its foreign debt, and took over private savings in bank accounts. Many thousands of people in the capital lost their jobs as companies and factories went bankrupt or lost their funding. The popular response was to try out different ways of fighting back: workers occupied factories and started to run them as co-operatives; neighbourhood assemblies sprang up to try to deal more democratically with local concerns; *cambalaches* or *trueques*, where people exchanged goods, became common; soup kitchens were set up; small local currencies were introduced that were widely accepted by shops and businesses.

As so often in recent history, the Argentine voters again turned to Peronism to provide a way out. From 2004 onwards, first Néstor Kirchner, and then after his untimely death his widow Cristina Fernández de Kirchner, have re-introduced more traditional Peronist economic policies to try to steady the ship. Several of the large firms privatized under President Menem were re-nationalized, including the national airline Aerolineas Argentinas, the oil company YPF and the postal service. Since the default on foreign debt, the Argentine government has been at loggerheads with the IMF and other multinational lending agencies, which Cristina Fernández says demonstrates her strong defence of the national interest. Paradoxically a large proportion of her government revenues have come, just as over the past centuries, from the export of agricultural products and of the mineral wealth that remained undiscovered by the Spanish settlers. Soy beans may to some extent have replaced wheat, and China taken over from Britain as the prime market for these exports, but the model does not seem to have changed. The fortunes of Buenos Aires and the national government continue to depend on the vagaries of this system. The country's wealth is still channelled and administered in the capital, and any conflicts that arise are soon felt on its streets and in its atmosphere.

Sometimes this happens quite literally: on one of my visits to the city, in April 2008, the centre was covered in a dense, acrid fog that kept many people indoors, while others ventured out only wearing face masks. Flights were cancelled at Aeroparque, and long-distance buses could not operate. But this was not a natural phenomenon: it came from producers around Buenos Aires deliberately setting fire to their crops in protest at Cristina Kirchner's attempts to increase government revenue by raising the taxes farmers had to pay on their exports. This particular crisis only lasted a few weeks, and as Argentina celebrated two hundred years of independence from Spain in 2010, it seemed as though Buenos Aires and the rest of the country could continue to enjoy stable, democratic government without the threat of a return to the dark days of military rule. But the city's inhabitants have learnt from bitter experience that the next storm is sure to be just beyond the horizon.

Jorge Luis Borges' first poetry collection,
published in 1923

5 | **The Written Word**
The City in Literature

Buenos Aires is a city dense with literary tradition. It has been written about since its foundation; its streets and buildings have aroused the imagination of generation after generation of writers. The great twentieth-century Argentine writer Jorge Luis Borges (1899-1986), a quintessential chronicler of the city, even went so far as to claim in *de Cuaderno San Martín* (1929) that it was:

> Hard to believe Buenos Aires had any beginning.
> I feel it to be as eternal as air and water.
> (*A mi se me hace cuento que empezó Buenos Aires:*
> *La juzgo tan eterna como el agua y el aire.*)

It is this kind of mythologizing of the Argentine capital that can lead other Latin Americans with longer and perhaps richer traditions to look askance at their Río de la Plata counterparts. The Mexican novelist Carlos Fuentes (who spent much of his childhood in Buenos Aires) wrote for example: "Buenos Aires needs to name itself, to know it exists, to invent itself a past, to imagine a future for itself: unlike Mexico City or Lima, a simple visual reference to the signs of historic prestige is not enough for it ... Could there be anything more Argentine than this necessity to verbally fill these empty spaces, to have recourse to all the world's libraries to fill the blank book of Argentina."

Yet this blank book was being filled almost from the start. As early as 1569 Luis de Miranda composed verses about the first city. Only 135 lines of the poem survive, and these were found and published as late as 1878. Contemplating the failure of Pedro de Mendoza's colony, he launched an idea that was to re-appear often in later centuries, portraying the Río de la Plata as an ungrateful widow, treacherous and disloyal, who destroys everyone and everything that tries to woo and conquer her.

Also from the sixteenth century is *Descripción y población de las Indias* by Fray Reginaldo de Lizárraga. Although it is not fiction, it includes powerful images. In his description of the port of Buenos Aires, the author writes that the 72 stallions and mares brought by Pedro de Mendoza in 1536 had multiplied so quickly that on the flat pampas they looked like brown mountains in the distance. From the earliest days of the foundation of Buenos Aires, the contrast between the port and the interior of Argentina was a favourite for writers. As the city grew in size and importance, the exploration of these differences became central to Argentine literature. One myth that found expression in *Siripo*, reputed to be the first non-religious drama written in Argentina (a verse play written in 1764 by Manuel José de Lavardén), was that of the captured white woman from the city taken by the "natives" in the pampas outside. Already in the eighteenth century the opposition between the "European" city and the "American" countryside beyond its boundaries is made plain. This myth of the abducted white woman reappears throughout the literature by Buenos Aires writers, from Esteban Echevarria in the nineteenth century to Jorge Luis Borges and the contemporary novelist César Aira with his 1981 *Ema la cautiva*. The city's one theatre, La Ranchería, burnt down a few years after *Siripo* was put on, to be replaced by the Coliseo. This theatre staged such pageants as the *Battle of Maipú*, or a re-creation of the last indigenous uprising in Peru entitled *Tupac Amaru* after the leader of the eighteenth-century revolt.

Early in the nineteenth century, as Buenos Aires and Argentina opened up to the world outside, it was accounts by foreign travellers that defined the city. Like many of these visitors, Charles Darwin, who arrived in 1833, was impressed by the area to the south of the port where the cattle driven in from the countryside were slaughtered:

The great corral where the animals are kept for slaughter to supply food to this beef-eating population is one of the spectacles best worth seeing . . . When the bullock has been dragged to the spot where it is to be slaughtered, the matador with great caution cuts the hamstrings. Then is given the death bellow; a noise more expressive of fierce agony than any I know: I have often distinguished it from a long distance, and have always known that the struggle was drawing to a close. The whole sight is horrible and revolting: the ground is almost made of bones, and the horses and riders are drenched in blood.

The ugly reality of the bloodletting on which the city's wealth has depended for centuries became an allegory for political violence in what is said to be the first published short story about Buenos Aires. *The Slaughteryard*, written by Esteban Echevarria in 1840 (but only published well after the end of Rosas' dictatorship) makes the link between the slaughter of cattle and political oppression in the murder of a young man pursued by members of Rosas' paramilitary *La Mazorca* (Corn Cob, which, as Norman Thomas di Giovanni, a recent translator of the story, claims, was the instrument used for the anal torture of their victims). This view of the city as a place of violence and death is also a recurring theme in the literature of Buenos Aires. At the same time, however, it was recognized as a centre of civilization, somewhere with a cosmopolitan outlook that was missing from the interior provinces of Argentina. For Domingo Faustino Sarmiento, the intellectual who became an early president of modern Argentina, the capital was the epitome of progress:

Buenos Aires is destined to become the greatest city in both the Americas. With a benign climate, mistress of the navigation of a hundred rivers that flow round her feet, softly reclining on an immense territory, and with thirteen interior provinces that have no other outlet for their products. She could be the American Babylon, were it not for the spirit of the pampas blowing through her, and the rich tributes of the rivers and provinces always pouring to her being drowned in her waters. She alone, in all the vast extension of Argentina, is in contact with the European nations; she alone can take advantage of foreign trade; she alone has power and money.

Buenos Aires was rapidly becoming the "Goliath's head on a puny body" that another writer, Ezequiel Martínez Estrada, described in his book of the same name in 1940. He, too, spoke of the soul of the city, which "although immortal as it should be, never-theless changes with the ages just as mankind's does". The tension between the capital and the provinces provoked literary as well as political disputes, but such was the capital's ever-increasing pre-dominance that nearly all aspiring Argentine writers headed there in the hope of being published, joining literary groups, or using it as a springboard to international recognition. In Sarmiento's *Facundo, civilización y barbarie* (1845), Argentina beyond the borders of the capital was seen as a "desert" (although in fact the pampas are one of the most fertile places on earth) inhabited by "savages" or by a mixed-race population that showed no respect for law and order. The iconic image of this was the *gaucho*, the cowboy of the pam-pas. Like his North American equivalent, the *gaucho* was only happy when riding out over endless unfenced land, or settling arguments through violence. The romantic version of *gaucho* life, idealizing open spaces and the nomadic lifestyle, is to be found in the epic poem *Martín Fierro* by José Hernández (published in two parts in 1872 and 1879); much of the literature of Buenos Aires has acted as a counterweight to this view of the essence of Argentina.

Urban Images

By the end of the nineteenth century there was a spate of novels portraying life in the booming capital, describing the riches and complexity of the society emerging there. An early account of how the upper classes in Buenos Aires struggled to cope with the economic downturn in the early 1890s is Julián Martel's *La Bolsa* (The Exchange). In the same way that the architecture of France was all the rage at the time, so Martel's novel aims to follow the precepts of Zola's "naturalism" in its sometimes xenophobic descrip-tions of frenetic *fin-de-siècle* urban life:

> The heart of the human circulation rushing through the streets of the centre of the city just as blood does through the veins, was the Exchange. All along the block next to the Exchange, along the strip that was left dry by the rain, one could see those parasites on our

wealth that immigration has brought to our shores from the remot-
est regions. Filthy Turks in their red fezes and torn slippers, with
their expressionless faces and loads of eye-catching goods; sellers of
gaudily-coloured prints; salesmen who had been forced to pack up
their wares but still harangued with their outlandish patter crowds of
idle passersby happy to stand in the rain to hear the virtues of marve-
lous inks or putty for fixing windows; beggars who stretched out the
stumps of their arms or showed off their rotting, useless legs, hoping
to arouse the public to pity; simple-minded women, some of them
beautiful, all of them in rags, dirty and dishevelled, many of them
entering the Exchange carrying purple-faced babies that looked fro-
zen and at the point of death, numbed by being given drugs obtained
by criminal means, the sight of whom led one to wonder who was
more repugnant and monstrous: the brutish mothers who used their
children in this way to receive some coins of charity, or the authority
which looked on indifferently out of ineptitude or lack of concern at
this scene of the most dreadful wretchedness, that turns to crime as
the only way out. The cries of the newspaper sellers echoed all round
the square. Ignoring the rain, protecting their papers under cloths,
they ran everywhere, climbed onto the trams, skipped across the road
crammed with carts and coaches of all kinds, always cheerful and
noisy, always ready to respond to any call. In short, that day Plaza
de Mayo was an extravagant, curious showcase of all the splendours
and miseries that go to make up the complex, hectic social life of the
great Buenos Aires.

As mass immigration transformed the city in the last years of
the century, so a new popular literature began to spring up, appearing in mass circulation magazines. Among these were the picaresque
tales by Roberto J. Payró (1876-1928), who launched a number of
stock characters, including the crafty *porteño* who always triumphs,
in tales such as *El casamiento de Laucha* (1906) or *Historias de Pago
Chico* (1920). It was around this time that the figure of the new
Italian immigrant began to make its appearance: hard-working,
family-minded, often cheated by fate from getting his just rewards.

The bastardized Spanish or *cocoliche* that many of these new immigrants spoke also found its way into literature, and especially into the pieces for theatre written from the turn of the century on, when *sainetes* or short melodramas were all the rage (similar in tone and emotional range to today's TV soap operas). These popular plays talked of life in the city's slums or *conventillos*, the drama of its streets and the debates going on in its bars and cafés. The playwright Alberto Vacarezza has provided a succinct outline of a typical *sainete* plot: "A tenement patio/an Italian man/a headstrong Spaniard/an attractive woman/a scheming man/two toughs with knives/an exchange of words/a fit of passion/a conflict/jealousy/an argument/a challenge/a stabbing/ high emotions/a shot, a call for help/the cops . . . the curtain."

Especially popular were the dramas written by the Uruguayan Florencio Sánchez (1875-1910). Plays such as *Canillita* (Paper Boy) reflected his anarchist principles while also initiating a tradition of sentimental portrayals of the big city's young outcasts that continued throughout the twentieth century. At the same time, the imagined conflicts of the *gauchos* out on the pampas became the subject of theatrical representation in the capital, just as their way of life was coming to an end. The first two decades saw a huge growth in the number of theatres: between 1910 and 1920 some thirty new ones were added to the already existing twenty. Although most performances were in Spanish, in the centenary year of 1910 there were more than four hundred plays given in Italian, more than a hundred in French, and scores in Yiddish. More than three million theatre tickets were sold in that year alone.

The instability and insecurity of the lives of the new arrivals was captured most memorably in the 1920s and 1930s in the novels, plays and the many *aguafuertes porteñas* (newspaper articles about the city and its characters) written by Roberto Arlt (1900-42), the son of immigrants from Germany and Trieste. In novels such as *El juguete rabioso*, *Los siete locos* and its sequel *Los lanza-llamas*, desperate dreams collide with sordid reality with often tragic results. His characters fantasize and plot in lowlife bars and cafés, wander the streets in search of a way out of the huge, oppressive city. The suicide scene in a bar near the port in *Los siete locos* (Seven Madmen, 1929) is so vivid that it still seems to have stamped its imprint on the area, as does the shooting of the "melancholy pimp" on Diagonal Norte near the Obelisk in the heart of the city. The language of Arlt's novels and short stories also reflects how those in an immigrant society use a Spanish language that is new to them: he often employs words for their sound rather than their meaning, creating a confusion that again is a vivid reflection of the cacophonic reality of the city streets in the early years of the twentieth century. As a journalist, Arlt wrote hundreds of sketches of Buenos Aires and its life in the 1920s and 1930s, describing individuals and many of the city's neighbourhoods with great accuracy and poignancy, as when he recalled suburban Flores at the start of the twentieth century:

> Flores was so spacious and beautiful in those days! Windmills were everywhere. Houses seemed not so much houses as mansions. Some of them are still there on Calle Beltrán or Ramón Falcón . . . these properties had coach-houses and in their courtyards, which were covered with wisteria, the chain of the bucket in the well set up its distinctive creak.

Two poetry groups also laid claim to expressing the essence of the burgeoning capital in the 1920s and 1930s. These were the Boedo poets and the group centred around the magazine *Martín Fierro*. The former, named after a *barrio*, insisted more on the political importance of art, while the latter, which included Jorge Luis Borges and Oliverio Girondo, placed greater emphasis on art for art's sake. Both groups saw the city as the inspiration for their work. From the early *Fervor de Buenos Aires* (1923) onwards, Borges returned again and again to the everyday life of its streets, in particular, as in Arlt's work, those of the neighbourhoods distant from the centre. As Borges wrote in *Evaristo Carriego* (1930), his book on the Argentine literary tradition, this was where he found the true beauty of the capital: "the unplanned and only real beauties of Buenos Aires are to be found in the suburbs—the lightness of the floating Blanco Encalada; the run-down corners of Villa Crespo, San Cristóbal Sur, or Barracas; the ruined majesty of streets around the La Paternal goods depot or Puente Alsina—all these are I believe more expressive than the works aimed at being deliberately beautiful: the Costanera, the Balneario, or the Rosedal."

Borges is possibly Argentina's best, and certainly best-known, twentieth-century writer. Many stories in his *Ficciones* and other books turn Buenos Aires into a mysterious, almost impenetrable labyrinth. Others, such as one of his most famous stories, *The South* (1953), encapsulate the drama of identity of the newcomers to the Argentine capital: "The man who landed in Buenos Aires in 1871 bore the name of Johannes Dahlmann and he was a minister in the Evangelical Church. In 1939, one of his grandchildren, Juan Dahlmann, was secretary of a municipal library on Calle Cordoba, and he considered himself profoundly Argentine. His maternal grandfather had been that Francisco Flores, of the Second Line-Infantry Division, who had died on the frontier of Buenos Aires, run through with a lance by Indians from Catriel; in the discord inherent between his two lines of descent, Juan Dahlmann (perhaps driven to it by his Germanic blood) chose the line represented by his romantic ancestor, his ancestor of the romantic death. An old sword, a leather frame containing the daguerreotype of a blank-faced man with a beard, the dash and grace of certain music, the familiar strophes of *Martin Fierro*, the passing years, boredom and solitude, all went to foster this voluntary, but never ostentatious nationalism."

Literature and Politics

In addition to celebrating Buenos Aires and Argentina, Borges, who was of English and Spanish ancestry, was keenly aware that his country's literature was an offshoot of the long European tradition. As such, in the 1930s he was an enthusiastic supporter of the influential Buenos Aires magazine *Sur*, founded by the "oligarchic" patron of the arts Victoria Ocampo. The magazine took a firmly internationalist line. It brought translations of the latest European and North American writers to Argentine readers; Victoria also invited international figures from Igor Stravinsky to Rabindranath Tagore, Antoine de Saint-Exupéry and Graham Greene to stay in her San Isidro villa. This cosmopolitanism and openness to the outside world, combined with conservative political views, brought the *Sur* group into increasing conflict with those writers, usually on the left, who thought that Argentines should look inward and write exclusively about their city and the country beyond it. What was a largely sterile conflict was exacerbated by the worsening political situation in the 1930s and 1940s. The theatre, for example, witnessed a growth of more politicized drama that rejected the conventions of the commercial stage and sought to challenge the society of compromise that grew up during what was popularly known as the "infamous decade". The Teatro del Pueblo (Theatre of the People) was founded in 1931 "to bring modern theatre to the masses, with the objective of bringing about the spiritual salvation of our people". It was at its most active from 1937 to 1943, when the new military government forcibly removed the company from its theatre in the centre of the city. It was not until more than forty years later that the Teatro del Pueblo was able to renew its regular performances, in a basement theatre off Avenida Corrientes.

The arrival in power of Colonel Perón in 1946 further divided writers and intellectuals. Some on the left saw his brand of populist nationalism as the authentic expression of Argentine identity, whereas more conservative writers in the capital rejected the values his movement expressed, seeing Peronism as stultifying and contrary to freedom of thought and expression. Borges and his fellow writers often met in cafés on central streets such as Calle Florida, and it was here that he and his great friend Norah Lange were arrested by the police in 1948 for singing the national anthem and demanding respect for the 1853 constitution. Later on, Borges was infamously removed from his post as director of the National Library and given a menial role as inspector of chickens at one of the capital's municipal markets. His old friend Victoria Ocampo was briefly jailed for "anti-Peronist" activities, and many other intellectuals also suffered under the new regime. These included one of the emerging stars of the new generation of writers, Julio Cortázar (1914-84), who left Buenos Aires in 1951 and never really returned. His works, though, and above all his masterpiece *Rayuela*

(1963), are steeped in the physical and emotional geography of the Argentine capital, even if in *62/Modelo para armar* (*62: A Model Kit*, 1968)) the city has turned into a nightmare: "I enter my city at night, I go down to my city where people are waiting for me or hurting me, where I have to flee from some terrible appointment, from what cannot be named, an appointment with fingers, with bits of flesh in a wardrobe, with a shower I cannot find, in my city there are showers, there is a canal which cuts my city in two and huge ships with no masts sail by in an intolerable silence towards a destination I know but forget on the way back, towards a destination that my city denies, because nobody embarks there, because this is where we stay, even though the ships pass by and from the smooth bridge of one of them somebody is staring at my city ..."

Imaginative evocations such as these contrast strongly with the views of Peronist writers such as Leopoldo Marechal (1900-70). His 700-page *Adan Buenosayres*, published in 1948, opens with a notable panegyric to the vibrant industrial city:

If you were able to fly like a bird and from the heights you could have looked down like a sparrow on to the city, I know your heart would have swelled with pride at the vision your loyal *porteño* eyes would have seen at that moment. Black, sonorous noisy ships anchored in the port of Santa María de los Buenos Aires, throwing onto unloaded decks at the wharves the industrial harvest of the two hemispheres, the colour and sound of the four races, the iodine and salt of the seven sea; at the same time, packed with the fauna, flora and mineral wealth of our land, tall, solemn ships left for the eight directions over the water, to the harsh farewell of naval sirens. If from there you had flown up the course of the Riachuelo to the site of the meat-packing plants, you would have been able to admire the commotion of steers and calves crowded together and bellowing in the sunlight while they waited between the posts for the hammer blow and skilful knife of the butchers, ready to offer their hecatomb to the world's voracity. Orchestral trains entered the city, or left for the jungles of the north, the vineyards of the west, the plains of the centre or the pastures of the south. From industrial Avellaneda to Belgrano in the north the metropolis is bound ringed by a belt of smoking chimneys that scrawl on the manly sky of the suburbs fervent declarations by Rivadavia or Sarmiento. The clatter of weights and measures, the tinkle of cash registers, conflicting voices and gestures clashing like weapons, rushing footsteps seemed to beat out the rhythm of the bustling city: here on calle Reconquista the bankers were playing the crazy wheel of Fortune; further on engineers as stern as Geometry were calculating the new bridges and highways of the world. Buenos Aires laughing as it starts working once more: Industry and Commerce led her by the hand.

In contrast to this hyperbolic view, writers such as Cortázar, Borges and his close friend Adolfo Bioy Casares (1914-99) continued to depict the city as a launch pad for mystery and fantasy. Borges converts the once smart residential suburb of Adrogué into something far more sinister in his story "Death and the Compass", while Bioy Casares created a parable for the political violence that was to engulf the city for several decades in his *Diario de la guerra del cerdo* (1969). Another Buenos Aires novelist, Ernesto Sábato (1911-2011), called the city "Babilonia", and his characters roam the streets from Barracas to Belgrano in search of chance encounters, epiphanies that might help them make sense of their urban lives.

By the 1960s, with repressive military governments and the emergence of left-wing guerrilla groups, many writers in Buenos Aires became increasingly politically engaged. Several of them, including the short story writer Rodolfo Walsh and the novelist Haroldi Conti, were later to pay with their lives for their political commitment, when they became two more in the list of thousands of Argentines killed by the security forces after the 1976 military coup. In the independent theatre, Osvaldo Dragún staged "revolutionary" dramas, while playwrights such as Ricardo Halac continued the tradition of social realism. Roberto Cossa also wrote about daily life among ordinary Argentines, although his most famous play, *La Nona* (The Granny, first performed in 1977) is a bitter farce reminiscent of the earlier *sainetes*. Cossa uses *lunfardo* or port slang to portray the "typical" Italian immigrant family whose members are desperately trying to free themselves from the despotic grandmother who dreams of being back in her childhood village in Italy and literally eats them out of house and home—a metaphor perhaps for the astronomical inflation that has so often eaten away at ordinary *porteños'* dreams of a better future. Cossa followed this success a decade later with *Yepeto*, which ran for more than 5,000 performances in a central Buenos Aires theatre. The turmoil of the last days of Peronism and the brutal military regimes that followed also led to playwrights such as Eduardo Pavlovsky (*El señor Galindez*) and Griselda Gambaro (*Los siameses, Ganarse la muerta*) to explore the psychological and existential reasons behind the violence and terror that surfaced in Argentina.

The violence of the 1970s, and more particularly of the years of military dictatorship from 1976 to 1983, saw many more writers forced to leave their beloved city for exile abroad. Some, like Humberto Costantini, wrote nostalgically of living in Mexico "5,000 kilometres from the Café La Paz" on Avenida Corrientes in central Buenos Aires, where writers and intellectuals used to gather early or late to debate literature and politics. Costantini (1924-87) wrote more directly of the years of terror in his novel *The Long Night of Francisco Sanctis*, published in 1984 shortly after his return to Buenos Aires after "seven years, seven months, and seven days" in exile. The novelist Manuel Puig (1932-90) wrote *The Kiss of the Spider Woman*, later made into a highly successful Hollywood film. Set in a Buenos Aires jail, the book consists of the conversations between Valentín, imprisoned for his Marxist political beliefs, and Molina, jailed for his homosexuality. Due to its controversial subject matter, the book was banned in Buenos Aires until 1983 and the return of democratic rule under Raúl Alfonsín. The myths of Peronism and the hold its two leaders had on many Argentines were explored in two novels by Tomás Eloy Martínez: *La novela de Perón* (1985) and *Santa Evita* (1995), while his later *The Tango Singer* plumbs the depths of a city where thousands of people can disappear without trace, apparently with no-one caring. Another writer forced into exile, Osvaldo Soriano, described the changes he saw in his fellow *porteños* when he returned to Buenos Aires in 1983 after a seven-year absence:

> One of the most distressing aspects for anyone returning from exile is to see how humiliated and guilty people feel. It is a matter which no outsider—and exiles are to some extent outsiders—can bear to touch on. Sooner or later, efforts at self-justification surface painfully. All those years of closing one's eyes to repression, the fraud of the Malvinas war, have left their mark, an infected wound, on the Argentine spirit. The military are now being attacked by public opinion, the press, and above all by those who until recently were their accomplices. It is astounding to read so many indignant articles, or to hear on the radio criticism from those who, only yesterday, were supporters of the regime. This "democratic opportunism" is as striking as the rout of the military.

Many younger Argentine writers have tried to come to terms in their literature with this violence of the 1970s and 1980s, while all are faced with a city around them that is constantly changing. Some authors, such as Sergio Bizzio or Martín Kohan, emphasize the moral degradation that has accompanied both the military regimes and the increase in everyday violence on the streets of the capital. Others like Alan Pauls try to capture the fragmentation and depoliticization of the new generation of *porteños*, no longer able to believe in anything and struggling to make their way in an often hostile environment. The poet Santiago Llach in his recent *Municipal Poems* reflects on the changing city around him:

> This Friday afternoon
> The children's playground
> Is full of kids and their mothers.
> The public is multicultural.
> Among the girls on the swings nearby
> There's one daughter of Bolivians,

Two with Peruvian parents
And two girls with Oriental features.
The mothers of the two Oriental girls
Are absolutely beautiful.
My daughter is blonde and blue-eyed.

The glory days of the Argentine publishing houses, when Buenos Aires took the lead in introducing writers censored in Franco's Spain or produced editions of new Spanish-language authors that were distributed throughout Latin America, have long since faded. The mainstream publishers are now subsidiaries of Spanish or multinational companies, generally following the fashion for "international bestsellers" and "airport fiction". Yet the Argentine capital continues to be a place of literary innovation, even if the number of readers has shrunk considerably. The bookshops along Avenida Corrientes continue to display their wares for late-night strollers, and there are many new literary cafés in both the centre and the *barrios*. New, and often ephemeral, literary magazines are published, and small publishing houses seem to mushroom in unlikely ways. For example, one took the lead from the *cartoneros*—the people coming into the centre of the city to recycle cardboard and other packaging as a way to make ends meet—by producing cheap editions of books bound in cardboard covers. Similarly, the independent theatre has also seen a revival in recent years. While the commercial theatres on Corrientes or Lavalle continue to draw in audiences with spinoffs from TV or musicals, there is a vibrant alternative drama scene that offers performances in private or abandoned houses or small theatres. Directors such as Vivi Tellas continue to experiment as they explore the stories and myths of the capital, as in *Disc Jockey* (2008): there can be as many as forty shows of this kind throughout the city at weekends.

6 | Visual Images
Art, Photography and Cinema

The very first visual image of the original settlement of Buenos Aires was an etching that accompanied Ulrich Schmidl's account of Pedro de Mendoza's failed expedition. This was published in Nuremberg in 1599, and shows a five-sided fort, with Mendoza's house as a solid two-storey building, surrounded by thatched huts and the figures of men with horses, or butchering cows. Five large canoes are drawn up on the banks of the "Rio della Plata oder Parana", while on a nearby hill dead bodies hang from gibbets.

This fanciful depiction is one of the few that survive, not only of the first settlement but of the successful second foundation. The Spanish colonial authorities did not allow any printing presses in the city, nor were there any engravers or indeed many known artists. The heritage of furniture, portraits and religious imagery from the colonial era is now largely to be found in the Enrique Larreta Museum of Spanish Art in Belgrano, surrounded by gardens in Andalusian style: one of the rare glimpses of almost three hundred years of history.

It was not until the early nineteenth century that foreign artists began to produce sketches and watercolours of the city in the early years of its independence from Spain. The English sailor and amateur painter Emeric Essex Vidal (born in Brentford in 1791) visited Argentina from 1816 to 1817. On his return to England, his sketches were worked up into watercolours and published in a set of 24 entitled *Picturesque Illustrations of Buenos Ayres and Montevideo* by one R. Ackermann. In his presentation of the album, Ackermann stressed the originality of the paintings: "The author of this work contented himself with sketching, originally without any view to publication, some of the characteristic features presented by the cities of Buenos Ayres and Montevideo, and such peculiarities in

An early (1900) photograph of Plaza de la Constitución
(Library of Congress, Washington DC)

the manners, customs, and habits of the people as appeared to him most striking during a residence of three years in the country. These delineations will, he presumes, prove the more acceptable to the curious in as much as, to his knowledge, no graphic illustration of these places has hitherto been submitted to the public." Essex Vidal was the first to show views of Plaza de Mayo and other street scenes inside the city, rather than viewing it from outside. He also painted the *mataderos*, *gauchos* chasing *ñandus* (rheas) and "typical" figures such as the *lecheritos*, the little boys selling fresh milk in the streets.

While Vidal concentrated on external scenes, the Swiss-born Charles Henri Pellegrini (father of a future president) was the first to make portraits of the society emerging in the newly independent Buenos Aires. An engineer by profession, he arrived in Argentina in 1828. The following year he sketched one of the city's leading ladies, Mariquita Sánchez de Thompson, in her literary salon. The result was so successful that over the next two years Pellegrini was commissioned to paint more than sixty portraits of the prominent men and women in Buenos Aires before the Rosas dictatorship forced many of them into exile. His paintings capture the increasingly extravagant styles of dress from that era, such as the enormous *peinetones* or hair-combs that were all the rage in the 1830s (also satirized in the lithographs of César Hipólito Bacle).

Picturing the City

The first known oil painting of the city, now kept in the Museo Nacional de Bellas Artes (National Art Museum), was also painted by a foreigner. This is *Puerto de Buenos Aires en 1834*, painted by the Scotsman Richard Adams. Originally brought to the Argentine capital in the early 1830s to help with the construction of the first Anglican church in the city (the newly independent republic had guaranteed freedom of worship, and the influential British community was quick to build both a church and a cemetery), Adams also painted watercolours that he later worked up in oils. His view of the port looks south from the riverbank back to the city on its hill. It is dominated by the new cathedral, the *cabildo* and the fort overlooking the river, but Adams also carefully includes the new Anglican place of worship, and put an Argentine flag flying high over Plaza de Mayo.

In the foreground he has also painted a variety of activities taking place on the low-lying banks of the Río de la Plata. On a cart with huge wheels a man is busy loading jars of fresh water to be carried up to the city. Near him two boys are fishing, and a train of mules is being led down to drink. In the middle background a group of black women have white washing spread out on the ground, while above them stretches the Alameda, the broad avenue skirting the river that was the first public promenade. The oil painting is clearly steeped in the atmosphere of eighteenth-century English or Dutch landscape painting. There is little exotic or strange about this city in the far south of the world: Adams' and later painters' assimilation of the Argentine capital to European traditions began a vast debate in Argentina about what a "national" representation of the country might involve.

The first Argentine-born painters of renown came in Buenos Aires during the 1840s and 1850s. Prilidiano Pueyrredón (1823-70) painted a striking portrait of Rosas' daughter Manuelita, dressed in the crimson that was the emblem of her father's violent rule, while Carlos Morel (1813-94) chose scenes of everyday life in *pulperías* (bars-cum-stores) and workplaces in the city and the pampas beyond.

Even in the mid-nineteenth century there were no official art schools in the Argentine capital. The first museum had been opened in 1812, when the ruling triumvirate, true to their Enlightenment ideals, had decreed that a natural history museum should be set up. In 1828 Bernardino Rivadavia extended this into the Museo Público, which included archaeological and historical exhibits together with paintings and sculptures. But it was not until 1878 that the Sociedad Estímulo de Bellas Artes was created, the precursor of modern art schools in Argentina, and 1895 before the Museo Nacional de Bellas Artes was founded. Its stated aims were "to save the most significant artistic manifestations of Argentine intelligence from oblivion and preserve them in time".

The gallery itself opened a year later, but since there was no building to house the collections, it at first occupied part of the Bon Marché department store on Calle Florida. Fifteen years later, the first Salon Nacional was held, and from then on the state bought many works from contemporary artists with the intention of building up a national collection.

As in most areas of cultural activity, French influence was dominant in Argentine painting when Buenos Aires and its economy were booming towards the end of the nineteenth century. Courbet and the Impressionists had many followers among young Argentine painters, who often visited, studied and exhibited in Paris. Among these was Eduardo Sivori, whose *El despertar de la criada* (The Maid's Awakening) from 1887 can be seen as the visual equivalent of the kind of social realism championed by Emile Zola and much imitated in artistic circles in Buenos Aires. Critics as the time complained that the picture was so crude that "you can see the corns on the poor girl's feet", but this new kind of intimate realism added a fresh dimension to portrayals of life in the burgeoning capital.

Other local artists brought Italian styles and interests to the Buenos Aires public: Ernesto de la Cárcova's *Sin pan y sin trabajo* (No Bread and No Work) shows a worker's family at a table bare of food, with a man pointing desperately out of the window at a distant view of factory chimneys where workers are striking and the police are about to move in and disperse them, while his wife looks on in despair.

It was the next generation of Argentine artists, from the early years of the twentieth century onwards, who began to question the predominance of a European-oriented way of depicting the world in art. Painters in the Nexus group, for example, wanted a specifically "Argentine" art. A painter like Pio Collivadino (1869-1945) studied in Milan but came back to live in La Boca, the port area of the city (one of his paintings of the Riachuelo is also in the Museo Nacional). His paintings from 1910 onwards often reflect the rapid changes in the city, from canvases portraying the novel tramways to new streets like the Diagonal Norte cutting through the city centre. Another artist, Martín Malharro, declared that "face to face with our country's nature, we need to imagine its mysteries, exploring, searching for the sign, the adequate means to represent it, even if that means distancing ourselves from all the precepts we have learned or acquired from such and such maestros, from this or that tendency."

As in literature, so different "schools" of artists began to form in Buenos Aires as the twentieth century progressed. One was known as the Florida group because its members met in the Confiteria Richmond on Calle Florida. (In 2011, much to the horror of traditionalists, the English-style Richmond was sold and is to be converted into a sports shop.) Painters such as Antonio Berni, Horacio Butler, Raquel Forner, Emilio Pettoruti and Lino Spilimbergo were prominent members of the group; they insisted above all on the formal, aesthetic values of art. A public reminder of their work is to be found nearby in the recently restored murals decorating the walls and ceilings of the Galerías Pacífico, a traditional shopping arcade also on Calle Florida.

One of the artists featured in the Galerías Pacífico frescoes is Antonio Berni (1905-81). Always concerned with social matters, in his later life he used cut outs and found materials to compose his pictures of life in the poorer areas of Buenos Aires. He created the character of a little boy and girl, Juanito Laguna and Ramona Montiel, who are the prototype of the capital's poor street urchins. Although sometimes over-sentimental and mawkish, Berni's images of the city and its inhabitants have maintained their popularity over the years, even after his death in 1981.

Perhaps the most interesting artist among those associated with the Florida group of painters was the highly eccentric Xul Solar (born Oscar Agustín Alejandro Schulz Solari). Rather than painting the reality of the city outside his studio window, Solar (1887-1963) invented fantasy worlds, combining interests in astrology, Buddhism and Oriental mysticism to create vibrant small watercolours that are close to the work of Paul Klee in spirit. Like his great friend Jorge Luis Borges, Xul Solar invested the flat, often prosaic spaces of the Argentine capital with a symbolic, fantastic dimension. He also invented several new languages, built innovative versions of the piano and compiled detailed astrological charts for friends. He was the model for the astrologer Schultze in Leopoldo Marechal's *Adán Buenosayres*, and appears in some of Borges' short stories. Nowadays his work can be appreciated in a new museum designed in the fantastic style of one of his own art works (the Xul Solar museum or Pan Klub at Laprida 1214).

Another circle of artists in 1920s Buenos Aires sought a more direct link between art and the political debates and social tensions then coming to a head and formed a group known as the Artistas del Pueblo. They produced mainly lithographs, engravings and woodcuts, considering these to be a cheaper form of art that could reach a wider public: many of their works were in fact displayed in the new public libraries, or in union offices and schools. Typical of their output and its emphasis on the life of the poorer people in the capital is *El Conventillo* by Guillermo Facio Hebequer (1889-1935), with shrouded figures huddled round in a bare, miserable room.

A third group of painters to emerge around this time was based in the port area of La Boca, among a largely Italian-immigrant community. The most famous of these was Benito Quinquela Martín

(1890-1977). Himself the son of an Italian, he worked in his father's coal-yard and took evening classes in art. He decided early on that he wanted to be a painter, and in 1917 won second prize in the influential Salon Nacional. His themes were almost always the port and its workers; although he painted the hardship of the dockers' lives, his palette was often bright and cheerful. As his fame grew, he helped found a school and an art museum that now houses many of his works and those of other painters of Buenos Aires, as well as a collection of ships' figureheads and port memorabilia. Quinquela Martín is also credited with restoring the Caminito, a gaudily painted street in La Boca lined with the original corrugated iron and wood immigrant shacks, which is now one of the city's main tourist attractions. Together with Quinquela Martín, Miguel Carlos Victorica (1884-1955) created poetic canvases out of the port's busy activities.

Following international trends, figurative art gave way to experiments in abstraction in 1940s Argentina. It was not until the 1960s that a new generation of figurative painters emerged, the most prominent being Rómulo Macció and Antonio Seguí. By now, the United States had a greater influence on emerging Argentine artists than France or Italy. An early exponent of "happenings" on the streets of Buenos Aires is Marta Minujín. In 1983, with the fall of the dictatorship, she created a temple of some 30,000 books banned by the military authorities as an eloquent protest against the lack of freedom of expression in Argentina. She is one of the artists whose more permanent works are to be found in the MALBA (Museo de Arte Latinoamericano de Buenos Aires), which opened just before the economic crash in 2001 and has become one of the most important cultural centres in the city, hosting popular exhibitions, cinemas and workshops. *Floralis Genérica*, the large metal rose sculpture outside the museum that opens and closes according to the weather conditions has already become one of the most recognizable symbols of the new Buenos Aires that emerged in the 1990s thanks to the policies of President Carlos Menem: clean, modern, powerful—until the next crash.

More recently still, a further stunning addition to Buenos Aires' museums has appeared in the form of the Colección de Arte

Amalia Lacroze de Fortabat. Housed in a huge gleaming hangar-like building in Puerto Madero, the new museum offers a collection of nineteenth- and twentieth-century Argentine art that rivals the rooms in the Museo Nacional. Although some of the displays are from ancient Greece and Egypt, as well as a Brueghel winter scene, a view of Venice by Turner and a room dedicated to portraits of the Fortabat family by a succession of renowned artists, the main thrust of the collection is a display of Argentine artists from Prilidiano Pueyrredón onwards. Many of the nineteenth-century paintings depict landscapes of the pampas and romanticized views of indigenous tribes, but there is also a comprehensive display of the different schools and tendencies in local art throughout the twentieth century. Rooms devoted to Buenos Aires artists such as Raúl Soldi and Antonio Berni, and a choice selection of many of the other prominent Argentine artists of the last hundred years.

Photography

It was the influential early painter Carlos Enrique Pellegrini who declared when one of his colleagues started to investigate the new fad for photographic daguerreotypes: "there is our enemy". From the 1840s onwards photography did indeed have a significant impact on the visual culture of the Argentine capital. Buenos Aires was still the "big village" when photography made its first appearance there. In 1843 John Elliot from the United States made the first daguerreotypes in the city. Some sources credit him with the very first Argentine photograph: a portrait of English-born Admiral Guillermo Brown with his wife Elisa Chitty, now kept in the Naval Museum in Tigre.

Elliot advertised in 1843 in the *Gaceta Mercantil* and the English-language *The British Packet & Argentine News* to "respectfully informs the public of Buenos Aires that he has just arrived from the United States with all the most up-to-date Daguerreotype machinery and is able to offer his services with regard to everything related to that admirable art to produce with the utmost brevity and accuracy portraits of all those who honour him with their trust and be so kind as to come to Recoba Nueva (Altos Number 56) plaza de la Victoria from the 26th June onwards when he will begin his work." He charged 100 pesos for a portrait, the equivalent of US$100 at the time: prices such as this put his work beyond the reach of all but the wealthiest in Buenos Aires society. Perhaps because of this, and due to the fact that many of the most liberal-minded members of Buenos Aires high society had fled across the Río de la Plata to Montevideo to escape Manuel Rosas' dictatorial ways, these new-fangled ideas did not catch on, with the result that Elliot appears to have given up and left after a year. Something similar seems to have happened with the second visiting professional photographer, John A. Bennet, "an artist from New York", who also set up a studio in the city centre for a few months, before disappearing from view.

Daguerreotypes were only in favour for a decade in the 1840s and 1850s, but some of the first views of the Plaza Victoria (nowadays the Plaza de Mayo), the *cabildo* and the old port were taken by another North American, Charles DeForest Fredricks using this process in the early 1850s. When daguerreotypes made way for wet plate photography on paper in the 1860s, the Italian immigrant photographer Benito Panunzi (1819-94) published his *Veduti de Buenos Aires* in 1865, now in the city's municipal library. These photographs have no artistic pretensions, but offer valuable historical evidence as to how the city looked before its massive expansion, showing for example the first version of the Teatro Colón on Calle Reconquista, the river and the new port installations. Like Elliot, Panunzi appears to have had a studio in Buenos Aires for only a few years, after which he moved on to an unknown destination. Around this time, it was another Englishman, Samuel Boote, who is credited with publishing the first postcards of scenes of Buenos Aires streets and also of the capital's middle classes taking weekend trips out to the more salubrious northern suburbs or to the islands of the Tigre Delta.

Among the first Argentine-born photographers was Juan Camaña, who also painted and had an artists' materials shop in the city centre, as well as being the French teacher to the dictator Rosas' daughter Manuelita. Another early professional photographer was Antonio Pozzo (1829-1910), who began as a portrait-maker but in the 1870s became one of the first to take photography out of the studio in order to capture images of the great events of the day.

It was when Buenos Aires became the capital of the new republic from 1880 onwards that photography became truly popular, offering well-off families studio portraits as well as albums of views of the city. The most renowned of these photographic studios was that of Alejandro Witcomb (born Alexander Witcomb in London in 1835). After arriving in Buenos Aires in 1878, he established his own Galería Witcomb on Calle Florida in 1880. His studio and art gallery soon made Florida the centre of the capital's artistic circles. Witcomb worked until shortly before his death in 1905, when his son took over the business, expanding it still further until 1945. The studio continued to exist, no longer run by the Witcomb family, until 1970, when more than 500,000 negatives were left to the nation. Over these years, the Witcomb studio compiled a vast social history of the capital and Argentine society. Until 1970, the Witcomb studio was also the official portrait-taker of Argentine presidents (his portrait of Domingo Faustino Sarmiento is one of his many masterpieces), and produced photographs of nearly all the leading members of high society as well as hundreds upon hundreds of views of daily life in the streets, the port, fiestas and so on.

Alongside the professional studios, the final years of the nineteenth century also saw the rapid growth of photography aficionados or dedicated amateurs. It was a lawyer, Francisco Ayerza (1860-1901), who in 1898 with a handful of others established the Argentine Amateur Photography Society, also in Calle Florida. These societies were hugely important for the history of photography in the city, as it was not until many years later that the subject began to be taught in art and professional colleges.

That same year witnessed the launch of *Caras y Caretas*, the first magazine in Buenos Aires to publish illustrations. For five decades, its photo-gravures and then photographs also offered a picture of the often dramatic events in the capital and beyond. Two daily newspapers, *La Nación* and *La Prensa*, also began to use photographs of current events to great effect. With the invention of the much less cumbersome Leica camera at the end of the 1920s, a new age of photo-journalism began in Argentina. Perhaps its most outstanding exponent was the young Juan di Sandro (1898-1988), who worked from the 1930s right up to the 1970s. His 1934 aerial shot of the visiting Graf Zeppelin airship offers a breathtaking view of the city, with its rectangles of streets and first skyscrapers clearly visible despite traces of early clouds of pollution. Di Sandro also captured boater-hatted crowds demonstrating in Plaza de Mayo and atmospheric night views of deserted damp streets with gleaming tram lines and peeling adobe buildings—the very essence of the nostalgia of tango.

Together with these often unacknowledged press photographers, in the 1930s the city welcomed an influx of talented refugees driven out of Europe by Hitler. Seeking refuge in the Argentine capital, they brought experimental approaches to photography, enriching the home-grown tradition. The Argentine-born Horacio Coppola and his German exile wife Greta Stern were foremost among those bringing these new ideas to Buenos Aires. Coppola produced portraits, near-abstract works, as well as what Sara Facio, herself a talented photographer and one of the foremost promoters of Argentine photography in recent years, describes in the following way:

> Coppola wanders through the city looking for corners, for the play of light in the daytime and at night, to seize that special climate which reflects an enormously attractive plastic vision. His style is clearly linked to the collective memory of the image of the 1940s, particularly his night-time shots, dense and mysterious and filled with tiny details that become symbols of the city.

For her part, Greta Stern brought wit and invention to the burgeoning industry of advertising photography, as well as her urban projects such as Patios de Buenos Aires. It was another female photographer, Annemarie Heinrich (born in Germany but raised in Argentina from the age of twelve), who made her name by photographing all the local film stars and celebrities. For more than forty years she provided the covers for the extremely popular *Radiolandia* weekly magazine, and in 1947 shot the first full colour front cover photograph in Argentina.

It is Sara Facio herself who succeeded in maintaining this rich photographic tradition through the difficult years of the 1970s and 1980s. Her photography gallery in the centre of the city, as well as the many publications of her Azotea photo-book publishing house, have survived economic and political crises, as well as frequent censorship. As early as 1966, for example, the book *Buenos Aires Buenos Aires* that she produced together with the writer Julio Cortázar was banned in Argentina because of comments Cortázar made about General Onganía's regime. Another photographic album (published by the University of Buenos Aires) that was hugely popular in the 1960s was *Buenos Aires, mi ciudad*, Sameer Makarius' nostalgic compilation on different neighbourhoods and special corners of the city. One of its texts though pointed to a growing problem, even at that time: "Buenos Aires is a city designed for the circulation of carriages and trams, which were the means of transport of the early century. For fifty years, nobody bothered to adapt the city to modern traffic. And by June 1962, our car factories were producing 10,000 vehicles a month . . . of the 800,000 automobiles licensed in Argentina, some 220,000 are from the capital. If we add another 35 per cent for all those registered in the adjacent province of Buenos Aires, that gives us the monstrous total of 300,000 vehicles whizzing around the city centre, shaving us so closely as we try to cross the streets that we acquire a new profile, and creating a deafening cacophony as they block one of the main arteries."

The 1970s presented a different problem for the photographers of Buenos Aires. Press cameramen suffered censorship and harassment. Several of those who were on the left of politics joined the ranks of the disappeared, while many more chose to leave Argentina for exile in Spain, Italy or any other country that would take them in. A haunting record of the city in this dark period is Andy Goldstein's *La muerte de la muerte* (The Death of Death), a reflection on death and memory that is all the more powerful for not containing any direct references to the ghastly events happening in Argentina at the time. Like many of his colleagues, Goldstein moved on from

1 The Argentine capital and the Río de la Plata from the air (Martin Terber/ Wikimedia Commons)

2 The Club de Pescadores/Fishermen's Club (Luis Argerich/Wikimedia Commons)

3 The Riachuelo and La Boca port (Nick Caistor)

4 The flat grasslands of the pampas (Luis Argerich/Wikimedia Commons)

5 Cattle on an *estancia*: the wealth of Argentina (Maximiliano Alba/Wikimedia Commons)

6 A nineteenth-century *gaucho* in traditional gear (Courret Hermanos Fotogs., Lima, Peru/Wikimedia Commons)

7 The Casa Rosada at the centenary of independence (Museo del Bicentenario)

8 The presidential balcony overlooking the 25 de Mayo square (Dziczka/Wikimedia Commons)

9 Almirante Brown's house near the Riachuelo (Wikimapia)

10 The historic *cabildo* or City Hall (Eurico Zimbres/Wikimedia Commons)

11 The Water Palace (HalloweenHJB/Wikimedia Commons)

12 Argentina's legislative Congress building (Fabián Minetti/Wikimedia Commons)

13 The Kavanagh building: Buenos Aires' first skyscraper (Phillip Capper/Wikimedia Commons)

14 The Palacio Barolo, inspired by Dante (Mgropius/Wikimedia Commons)

15 The 'English Tower' by Retiro railway station (Phillip Capper/ Wikimedia Commons)

16 The Recoleta cemetery (Andrew Currie/Wikimedia Commons)

17 The obelisk, at the heart of the city (Alex Proimos/Wikimedia Commons)

18 The Avenida 9 de Julio (w:es:Usuario:Barcex/ Wikimedia Commons)

19 The Caminito in la Boca neighbourhood (Humawaka/Wikimedia Commons)

20 Carlos Gardel, Evita and Maradona in La Boca (Photo by Adam Jones adamjones. freeservers.com)

21 Painted wooden houses in La Boca (Luis Argerich/Wikimedia Commons)

22 Pedro de Mendoza, the first founder of Buenos Aires (Belgrano/Wikimedia Commons)

23 Manuel Belgrano, hero of the independence struggle (Mushii/Wikimedia Commons)

24 Bartolomé Mitre, general and president (Poco a poco/Wikimedia Commons)

25 César Hipólito Bacle's satire on Buenos Aires fashion in the 1830s

26 The dictator Rosas' daughter Manuelita portrayed by Prilidiano Pueyrredón (Google Art Project)

27 Juan Manuel Rosas in 1840, painted by Cayetano Descalzi (Museo Histórico Nacional)

28 President Juan Domingo Perón and Eva Duarte de Perón at the height of power and fashion in 1948 (Museo del Bicentenario)

FORJADOR DE LA NUEVA GRAN ARGENTINA

29 Evita as a candidate for canonization after her death in 1952 (Wikimedia Commons)

30 Perón, the creator of the new Argentina, 1947 (Museo del Bicentenario)

31 The *bandoneón*, soul of the tango (Pavel Krok/Wikimedia Commons)

32 Tango in the streets of Buenos Aires (Michael Clarke Stuff/Wikimedia Commons)

33 A statue of Carlos Gardel outside the Abastos market, where he grew up (JOPARA/Wikimedia Commons)

34 Luna Park, Buenos Aires' "palace of sports" (Leandro Kibisz/Wikimedia Commons)

35 Boca Juniors Football Club . . . (Zweifüssler/Wikimedia Commons)

36 . . . and their rivals, Club Atlético River Plate (Julieta Mancuso Villar/Wikimedia Commons)

37 Domingo Faustino Sarmiento, intellectual and president (Ezarate/ Wikimedia Commons)

38 Jorge Luis Borges, fabulist of Buenos Aires, 1978 (Wikimedia Commons)

39 The writer Victoria Ocampo's famous villa on the outskirts of the city (Beatrice Murch/Wikimedia Commons)

40 Meat for everyone: a traditional *asado* (Gdiaz/Wikimedia Commons)

41 The Argentine Pope Francis I with President Cristina Fernández de Kirchner and a *mate* gourd (casarosada.gob.ar/Wikimedia Commons)

42 The traditional Café Tortoni on Avenida de Mayo (Ferchulania05/ Wikimedia Commons)

43 Martín García Island in the estuary of the Río de la Plata (Wikimedia Commons)

44 Punta del Este, holiday playground in neighbouring Uruguay (Roberto Tietzmann/ Wikimedia Commons)

45 Colonía del Sacramento, across the estuary from Buenos Aires (HalloweenHJB/Wikimedia Commons)

46 Tierra Santa, the Holy Land theme park near Buenos Aires (Laura Valerga/ Wikimedia Commons)

snapping daily events to producing books of photographic essays. Some of the most memorable of these volumes by photographer Adriana Lestido: her portraits of women in the jails of Buenos Aires show a very different side of urban life.

Writing at the end of the 1990s, Sara Facio summed up the situation for contemporary photographers in Buenos Aires in the following way: "From 1970 on, it was impossible to go round the streets with camera bags and accessories. Simply to stop and observe people, streets, or objects with time and calm was to arouse suspicion. So it is only in the last decade that photographers have abandoned a purely documental vision—one almost forced on them by circumstances, and replaced it with a freer gaze. Nowadays photographers show us social themes they want to give their opinion about, deliberately chosen by them because they are stirred by them and feel involved in them. They deal with these topics in a personal way, without prejudice or hypocritical euphemisms. They also allow themselves to escape and explore their own interior worlds, allowing fantasy to rise to the surface."

Plebeian Palaces: Cinema

Another technological import that quickly gained acceptance in the Argentine capital was the cinema. Thanks to the cultural affinities between Buenos Aires and France at the end of the nineteenth century, it was not long before the pioneering efforts in this new medium found their way across the Atlantic. In 1896, less than a year after the Lumière brothers' first films were shown in Paris, they appeared in Buenos Aires. The next year, French immigrant Eugenio Py is credited with filming the first short feature made in Argentina: *La bandera argentina* (The Argentine Flag). The first dramatic film was produced a decade later, and related an episode from 1820s Argentine history: *El fusilamiento de Dorrego* (The Shooting of Dorrego). Over the next few years, film labs, studios and, of course, cinemas were built in the capital: there were huge audiences for the first full-length feature, *Amalia*, based on the novel by José Mármol and directed by Enrique García Velloso. This was followed by another adaptation from literary sources, *Nobleza gaucha*, which in 1915 became the first film from Argentina to be exported throughout Latin America. Two years later, the first of a long line of "tango" films was made: *El tango de la muerte* showed the hardships of life among the immigrant communities. Argentines also like to claim that the first full-length animated feature in the world was made in Buenos Aires. This was *El apóstol*, a satirical view of Hipólito Yrigoyen's presidency that used the lower-class *lunfardo* dialect in its titles and the streets of the capital as a convincing backdrop. The links between Argentine cinema and politics were once again stressed in 1919 with two films, the drama *Juan sin ropa* and a documentary portraying the events of the *semana trágica* or 'tragic week' (see p. 64).

The 1920s was a decade of growing audiences and the construction of a large number of "picture palaces", but there was also the increasing predominance of films imported from Hollywood. Even so, more than a hundred feature films were made in Buenos Aires, while Federico Valle began a weekly national newsreel: *Film Revista Valle*. But it was the advent of sound in the cinema at the start of the 1930s that led to a golden period for the Buenos Aires based Argentine film industry. José Agustín Ferreyra again depicted working-class life in the capital in *Muñequitas porteñas*, while tango, especially thanks to the international idol Carlos Gardel, found renewed popularity in another medium. By the mid-1930s Argentine studios (almost exclusively situated in or around the capital) were pouring out more than 25 films a year, establishing their pre-eminent position throughout Latin America. As Tim Barnard points out in his *Chronology of Argentine Cinema*, this predominance was due to the sheer variety of genres being made: 'tangos ... the "social-folkloric" genre ... historical films and gaucho epics ... crime thrillers ... urban dramas ... "women's" melodramas ... comedies ... and literary adaptations (including a sound remake of *Amalia*)".

Cinema in 1930s Buenos Aires inevitably drew its huge audiences from people who wanted to escape the often difficult reality of everyday life for the glamour and escapism offered by film. Jorge Luis Borges, who during this decade was one of Argentina's foremost cinema critics, put this succinctly in one of his pieces in the magazine *Sur*: "to go into a cinematograph on Calle Lavalle and find myself (rather to my surprise) in the Bay of Bengal or on Wabash Avenue seems to me to be far more preferable than to go into that same cinematograph and find myself (rather to my surprise) in Calle Lavalle." As Edgardo Cozarinsky points out in his book on the capital's cinemas, *Palacios plebeyos* (People's Palaces), the buildings themselves tried to take the spectators out of the often depressing reality outside: "In the concept of the movie palace, both the cinema and all its services had to be designed to make the client feel like a member of an imagined nobility. As a spectator, he could gain access to a kingdom that no monarch of the past had enjoyed: the world of the cinema."

Many of these movie palaces were built along the central street of Calle Lavalle, or on Avenida Corrientes. They drew huge crowds night after night in the 1930s to see such local stars as Libertad Lamarque, Tita Morello or the comedian Luis Sandrini. The Gran Opera, in the most kitsch Art Deco style, was perhaps the grandest of the cinemas. Indeed, so grand and kitsch was it that the arbiter of good taste in mid-twentieth-century Argentina, Victoria Ocampo, complained in her magazine *Sur*: "Lately, the most terrible of all these nightmares showed above our heads a starry night, with clouds, and surrounded us with a marvellously dreadful city full of towers the colour of meringue, balconies, and statues." Her preference was for the other huge cinema opposite, the Gran Rex, which obeyed her modernist preference for simple lines, lack of decoration and moderation inside as well as out. Neither of these Art Deco creations still functions as a cinema: both have become places where big concerts or musical reviews are staged. Many other Buenos Aires "movie palaces", especially in the outer neighbourhoods, have now been taken over by evangelical sects, offering a different kind of escape from the world around them.

It proved more difficult for the Argentine film industry, still based almost exclusively in Buenos Aires, to stand apart from the political events of the 1940s. US governments saw Argentina's neutral stance during the Second World War as in fact favouring the countries of the Axis. In reprisal, they embargoed the sale of raw film stock for filmmaking. As a result, Argentine producers turned to the new strong man Juan Domingo Perón for protection and support for the industry. His response was to keep ticket prices as low as possible to encourage attendance, and to legislate for quotas on Argentine films to be shown in cinema programmes (one week every two months had to be dedicated to nationally made films), while at the same time establishing control over what he saw as a valuable means of spreading propaganda for his regime. Edgardo Cozarinsky remembers a less politically charged consequence of one of Perón's nationalist moves: the "live show" decreed by the first Peronist government provided a refuge for variety artists, many of whom were out of work or in decline. "This show lasted between ten and fifteen minutes; its quality depended on the cultural level to which the cinema aspired. In the Gran Opera, for example, it was generally performed by Charles Wilson, who sat at the organ in his glittering evening dress and played arrangements reminiscent of Ethel Smith's in the MGM comedies. In the poorer neighbourhood cinemas one could find magicians whose rabbits stubbornly refused to come out of their hats, or the flamenco group whose stamping feet went right through the rotten stage-boards."

The period after Perón's downfall in 1955 encouraged a new generation of filmmakers who were no longer content to produce escapist melodramas or nationalistic epics. The films of Leopoldo Torre Nilsson brought adaptations of Borges, Bioy Casares and Manuel Puig to the screen, as well as psychological dramas of the urban middle classes he saw around him. In the 1960s Argentine cinema was becoming radicalized in the face of censorship and political polarization. While the mainstream continued to churn out cheap comedies and melodramas showing a vision of Buenos Aires far removed from reality, the directors of the Cinema Liberación movement wanted film to be a revolutionary tool. *La hora de los hornos* (The Hour of the Furnaces), a film directed by Fernando Solanas and Octavio Getino in 1968, was the manifesto of this movement. The filmmakers declared that "Latin America is a continent at war" and showed striking montages of current repression in Buenos Aires and other cities together with historical images to demonstrate how British and US imperialism had turned Argentina into a neo-colonialist fiefdom ruled over by the local "oligarchy".

Despite attempts to create a revolutionary cinema, the film industry in Argentina was badly affected by the economic and political chaos of the first half of the 1970s. Many neighbourhood cinemas closed down: even the grander outlets in the city centre suffered from lack of investment and insufficient funds to be able to import Hollywood hits, with the consequence that Calle Lavalle became a sad shadow of its former glitzy self. One of the rare successes for Argentine cinema came in 1975 when director Lautaro Murúa brought out *La Raulito* (Tomboy Paula), a downbeat picture of life in the city's slums that starred Marilina Ross as the young girl who has to disguise herself as a boy to survive, and in the end succeeds in escaping to the comparative haven of the seaside resort Mar del Plata.

The 1976 military coup only accelerated the process of decline in the cinema, as a climate of fear greatly reduced audiences while many of the left-wing directors, actors and writers fled abroad in exile. There was little finance available for those who remained, so Argentine production was often reduced to soft porn or outdated farce. The economic policies of the military governments opened Argentina up to foreign imports, and it became far easier in these years to see the latest films from Hollywood than anything that gave audiences the chance to reflect on what was going on in their own society.

This process was to some extent reversed with the return of civilian rule in 1983-84. A film such as *La historia oficial* by Luis Puenzo was the first and perhaps hardest-hitting criticism of the savagery that had been unleashed under the military. Fernando Solanas returned from exile to continue with a long Argentine tradition, shooting *Tangos: el exilio de Gardel* with music by the great composer Astor Piazzolla in Paris and Buenos Aires. This provided yet another bitter-sweet reflection on how far the Argentine capital, which once considered itself as elegant and thriving as the French one, had fallen by the last quarter of the twentieth century.

With the economic boom of the 1990s, many young filmmakers again began to invest time and money in portraying contemporary life in Buenos Aires. Most of these directors had a background in advertising, and this showed in both the sophisticated handling of cinematic techniques and in the new "cool" of dialogue and atmosphere. Typical of this new, self-aware cinema was the 2000 film *Nueve reinas* (Nine Queens), which won audiences not only in Argentina but all round the world. Written and directed by Fabián Bielinsky, it follows the adventures of two conmen in Buenos Aires, while offering a satirical take on the "new rich" of President Menem's Argentina and showing *nouveau riche* districts such as Puerto Madero being built. At the same time, these sharp anti-heroes, who are never quite as clever as they think they are, take the spectator back to the traditional figures of the *criollo* pimps and *compadritos* who had long been a mainstay of tango. Another film that won international awards and showed life in a run-down Buenos Aires suburb was the 1999 *Mundo grúa* (Crane World) directed by Pablo Trapero. Shot in black-and white, the film was an attack on the huge gap between rich and poor in contemporary Argentina, and the way in which the urban working class had been left out of the new prosperity. Meanwhile, Martín Rejtman's minimalist comedies of manners such as *Los guantes mágicos* (Magic Gloves) memorably portray the neuroses and obsessions of the urban middle classes.

As ever, though, the Argentine film industry has suffered from the lack of economic stability in the country. The economic crash of 2001-02 threw national cinema into disarray yet again, but young directors have once more reacted with panache and great creativity. Daniel Burman, for example, has directed a trilogy, *Esperando al Mesías* (Waiting for the Messiah, 2000), *El abrazo partido* (Lost Embrace, 2004) and *Derecho de familia* (Family Law, 2006) which cast a wry glance at Jewish identity in Buenos Aires with a lightness of touch that has often been compared to Woody Allen.

This new generation of filmmakers has benefitted from a levy on foreign films distributed in Argentina: it is an ironic fact that most Argentines seem to prefer to watch Hollywood or other foreign-made films, but in so doing are helping to pay for often more challenging work by native-born directors, actors and technicians. At the same time, the comparatively low cost of filmmaking in Buenos Aires has led to a number of big international productions being made there in recent years, including the much reviled (in Argentina) film adaptation of the musical *Evita*. This production boom even led Francis Ford Coppola (*The Godfather*, *Apocalypse Now*) to come to live and work in the city. In 2009 he released his own feature on life in Buenos Aires, centred round generations of an Italian immigrant family: *Tetro*. In the words of one its kindest critics: "it was so bad it was good."

Antonio "Gaucho" Blasi (1922-2007), tango composer, band leader and accordionist (Lucasajus/Wikimedia Commons)

7 | Tango
The Sound of the City

A restaurant in La Boca, on a Friday night. The food is Italian, served on long tables with red check tablecloths and wooden chairs. As well as pasta there is the inevitable steak, and the rough Argentine wine with so much tannin that it almost takes off the roof of your mouth. The clientele are ordinary *porteños*, couples or families with children seemingly of all ages: in Buenos Aires the smaller ones are not seen as a nuisance, but are welcomed, fussed over by customers, waiters and owners alike. It is getting late, around midnight, when suddenly from behind the bar the music of a tango starts up. Roused from their stupor, the older couples are the first to get up and dance. More reluctantly, with a stiff self-consciousness, some of the younger customers get to their feet too, and before long the whole restaurant is full of couples shuffling along, the men holding themselves erect, left hand cupped round the women's outstretched hands, the other resting lightly in the middle of their backs—the more refined (or sweatier) of them delicately draping a handkerchief over their right hand. There is no ceremony, no showing-off, and people drop out when they feel they have had enough, returning to their families and more wine.

The midnight dancers in La Boca are bringing tango back to the corner of the city where it first began. There are many theories about how exactly tango was born, and even about the meaning of the word itself. Some say it is onomatopoeic for the sound of an African drum: the only problem with this suggestion being that there are no drums in tango music. Others argue that it comes from the Portuguese verb *tangere*, to touch, but again this was certainly not one of the outstanding characteristics of early tango dances. The most likely origin of the word appears to be from an African language, meaning an enclosed space where people danced.

Whatever its etymology, it seems certain that tango first emerged in the booming immigrant city of the 1870s and 1880s.

The growing numbers of port workers, soldiers returning from the wars against Paraguay and the remaining black inhabitants of the poorer areas of La Boca and Bajo Palermo made this a thriving area for brothels of all kinds. While the customers were waiting, they were entertained by small groups of musicians, usually playing a piano, guitar and a violin. The music was a mixture of Spanish *habaneras*, tunes from the *milonga* dance music of the Argentina countryside, and black carnival rhythms.

The first tango dancing, often between two male customers, has been described as "a rhythmic pantomime of the sexual act". This same description apparently holds true more than a century later, as the novelist Tomás Eloy Martínez writes in his book *The Tango Singer*: "the dance began with a somewhat brutal embrace. The man's arm encircled the woman's waist and from that moment she began to back away. She was always on the retreat. Sometimes he arched his chest forward or turned side-ways, cheek to cheek, while his legs sketched tangled figures that the woman would have to repeat in reverse . . . It looked like athletic sex, tending towards perfection but with no interest in love."

Alongside the dance and the often pornographic lyrics accompanying it, a whole myth of tango life began to grow up. The protagonists of this narrative were the prostitute (usually with a heart of gold, who would listen to her customers' melancholy complaints and offer both physical and spiritual solace), the *madame* running the brothel (the keeper of order and authority) and the pimp, the *rufián* (who soon had as many aliases as his diverse origins, from *canfinflero* to *cafisho* to the splendid *enjailaifero*, the enjoyer of the high life). Around the turn of the twentieth century, these pimps became popular heroes, their "hat worn rakishly over the ear, silk tie with pearl tie-pin, rings on every finger, often worn over a pair of white kid gloves, a vicuña poncho over the shoulders, spats and kid boots so soft they could be folded and put in the pocket" as Blas Matamoro has it. The *rufián* was a peculiarly melancholic figure (he did not have to do any of the work) who adopted a fatalistic attitude towards life in general. One of the most famous of these early "tango heroes" was Eduardo Arolas. A tango musician as well as a pimp, he fell in love with "La Chiquita", whom he apparently adored and went so far as to marry. Inevitably, this being the tango world, La Chiquita betrayed him with his best friend. Arolas turned to drink, and eventually quit Buenos Aires for Paris, where he died one autumn night in 1924 from stab wounds in a fight with the French pimps known as *maquereaux.*

Arolas was known as the "tiger of the bandoneon", and it is this strange instrument that quickly became an integral part of tango music and legend. The *fuelle,* or "squeeze-box" as it is commonly known, was brought to Buenos Aires in the 1870s by German seamen. It is definitely not an accordion: the Wikipedia definition gives some idea of the complexity of the instrument: "unlike the piano accordion, the *bandoneón* does not have keys as per a piano, but has buttons on both sides. Additionally the notes produced on push and pull are different (bisonoric). This means that each keyboard has actually two layouts: one for the opening notes, and one for the closing notes. Since the right and left hand layouts are also different, this adds up to four different keyboard layouts that must be learned in order to play the instrument. However, there is the advantage that the notes tend to progress from the bass clef on the left hand to above the treble clef on the right. To make matters even more confusing, there are bandoneons that are monosonoric (same note on push and pull). These variants are more compatible with a chromatic tuning structure."

This complex structure gives the instrument its unique wheezing, staccato sound that seems specifically made for the melancholy, melodramatic swoops of both tango dancing and its lyrics. Few of the words to the earliest songs have survived, but an early example *Dame la lata* (Give me the Token) clearly shows its origins. The *lata* or token was paid for by the client, then handed to the girl, who at the end of the day had to submit all of them to her *cafisho* or the *madame* to check against her earnings. (The expression is still to be found in *porteño* slang, *no me des lata* meaning "don't give me any trouble".)

In the first years of the twentieth century, tango music gradually moved out of the brothels, first to cafés in the same neighbourhoods, the *orillas* or margins of the city, and then to dance academies. As it did so, the musicians became more professional and the groups became larger: five or six people, including two violins and often a clarinet. Tango music also soon came to feature in the *sainetes*, comic operas that replaced the Spanish tradition of *zarzuelas* in the popular theatres springing up in Buenos Aires. At the same time, upper-class youths caught on to the craze, and often visited the dancehalls for the music or to cause trouble with the workers who were the usual audience.

Carlos Gardel

It was around the time of the centenary of independence, in 1910, that tango is said to have truly been accepted in wider Buenos Aires society. In 1912 the renowned Baron Antonio Demarchi held what is reputed to have been the first high society tango dance in the Palais de Glace in the "aristocratic" *barrio* of La Recoleta, while cabarets such as Hansen and Armenonville became *the* place for the upper classes to be seen. It was in the latter that perhaps the greatest figure in tango of all time first began to make his name: Carlos Gardel. Known as "the South American song thrush", his life is still surrounded by a thousand myths. The first of these concerns where he was born: for many years, he himself claimed this was across the river in Uruguay; others maintained that he was such a central figure to the music of Buenos Aires that he must have been born there. The truth is that he was born in Toulouse, in the south-west of France, on 1 December 1890, and given the name Charles Romuald Gardes. His mother, Berthe or Berta as she became known in Argentina, was not married, and the stigma of bearing a child out of wedlock appears to have been what drove her to emigrate two years later to the Argentine capital. So from the very start, the young Charles—or Carlos, as he was soon renamed in Buenos Aires—was living the tango. As a boy, he shared one room with his mother in the working-class area around the city's main fruit and vegetable market, the Mercado de Abasto. (A magnificent Art Deco building was constructed in the 1930s to house the market. It fell into disrepair in the 1980s when the main market was moved to the outskirts of the city, and then in the 1990s became yet another shopping mall. The area around it remains a centre for late-night tango.)

More myths surround Gardel's early life: he is said to have worked as a conductor on a tram, to have been a petty thief and to have spent time in prison. But by the second decade of the twentieth century, he was making a living as a singer. From his first great success, *Mi noche triste* (My Sad Night), composed in 1916 by Pascual Contursi, he never looked back. The title shows how by this time tango was firmly associated with sadness and loss, and a nostalgic view of life that has often been linked to the sense of exile felt by the hundreds of thousands of newly-arrived immigrants who felt cut off from their roots back in Europe. In this sense, it has been called the "blues of Buenos Aires", although the suffering it expresses is more in the mind than the real oppression suffered by the black population of the United States.

Gardel was lucky enough to come on the scene just when the first records were being produced, and when new "cinema palaces" were opening to show highly popular silent films. He first appeared in one of the early successes, *Flor de Durazno* (1917), singing songs that were reproduced from records in the cinemas, or interpreted there by a tango orchestra.

By the end of the second decade of the twentieth century, tango was not only the rage across Buenos Aires and the rest of Argentina, but was danced with equal passion in Madrid, London, New York and Paris. As so often in Argentine history, international success in Paris, the place that many wealthy Argentines regarded as their spiritual home, cemented its reputation back home. It also meant that singers such as Gardel could become international stars. In the 1920s he began singing, making records and starring in films in France and then in New York. One of his biggest successes was the 1934 song *Mi Buenos Aires querido* (My Beloved Buenos Aires), taken from a film of the same title:

My beloved Buenos Aires
When I see you again
There'll be no more sorrow or forgetting ...

This is the quintessential nostalgia of the *porteño*: he probably has to leave the city to seek to better himself because his expectations there have not been fulfilled, and yet he can only feel happy and complete when he is back in the port, remembering how much simpler life used to be.

El farolito de la calle en que nací
fue el centinela de mis promesas de amor,
bajo su quieta lucecita yo la vi
a mi pebeta, luminosa como un sol.
Hoy que la suerte quiere que te vuelva a ver,
ciudad porteña de mi único querer,
y oigo la queja
de un bandoneón,
dentro del pecho pide rienda el corazón.

The little street lamp, standing on my native street,
Was there to witness my first promises of love.
Its quiet light was shining when I went to meet
My lovely sweetheart, glowing like the sun above.
Now that my fortune has me seeing you once more,
The only city that I've ever hankered for,
Hearing the plaintive
Bandoneon,
My heart inside me wants to break out on its own.

The setting is not that of the centre of the city, but one of the poorer neighbourhoods, lit by a "'little streetlight"—and the girl he loves is a *pebeta*, *porteño* slang or *lunfardo* for a young girl (also *papusa*, *mina* and many more expressions) and originally meaning a bread roll. But although the song speaks of the "only city I've ever hankered for", in one revealing interview from around the same time, Gardel expressed the ambivalence many creative artists have felt towards their city:

After a few months in Buenos Aires, I get an irresistible urge to leave ... It seems I am a vagabond, never content with my fate ...

> Buenos Aires is very nice, *che*, and its Calle Corrientes has an inde-
> finable enchantment that binds us with links of steel . . . But when
> you have known Paris, when you have seen the Côte d'Azur, when
> you have enjoyed the applause of royalty, it doesn't quite satisfy . . .

This nostalgic love song to the city became even more poignant
when in 1936 the *Troesma* (*vesre* or back slang for *maestro*) was killed
in an air crash in the distant country of Colombia. Gardel's body was
flown back to Buenos Aires for burial. In 1937 a larger than life-size
bronze statue to him was unveiled in Chacarita cemetery. Fans of the
singer still make sure that he is always casually holding a lighted ciga-
rette in his right hand and wearing a red carnation in his buttonhole.
The inscription on the statue reads: "Carlos Gardel, singing better
every day." No other figure in tango has given rise to such a legend
and such devotion across generations of *porteños* as Carlos Gardel.
The Argentine sociologist Juan José Sebreli has suggested in *Buenos
Aires, vida cotidiana y alienación* (1964) that his popularity "is the
symbol of the hallucinatory dreams of underdogs, who hate the rich
because they cannot themselves be rich. He is someone who has 'arrived' and, by arriving, has taken revenge for all those who never could
or did. He is someone who has risen from the tenements of Abasto to
the dazzling banqueting table of the great international bourgeoisie."

An Evolving Genre

Gardel, other singers and the newly professional tango orchestras benefitted enormously from coinciding with the explosion of
new media in the 1920s and 1930s. Sheet music and records sold
in thousands of copies. The radio began to broadcast tango concerts. The first proper sound film made in Argentina was entitled,
naturally, *Tango* (1933) followed by *Dancing* in the same year, and
El alma del bandoneón (The Soul of the Bandoneon), from 1935. By
this time, the music was no longer played intuitively, but had begun
to be classified. The *orquesta típica* consisted of two violins, two bandoneons, a piano and a guitar or double bass. New rhythms were
explored, and the influence of North American jazz made the music
ever more urban.

The lyrics of these tangos were largely based around stereotypical characters and situations, as the Argentine social historian Blas Matamoro explains:

> ... the *milonguita* (girl-next-door) who betrayed her neighbourhood for a silk gown, and now pretends she is French in the private rooms of expensive cabarets; the pure, good mother who lives in poverty and has to suffer neglect from her wastrel sons. She never complains or rebels, but always understands and forgives. The lower class youth who is maintained by a whore and claims to be rich or a well-off gringo; the rich kid who thinks he is superior because he has an inheritance. Then there is the cabaret, a place of temptation and perdition, and the neighbourhood, which protects and saves.

The political and economic difficulties of the 1930s gave rise to any even more world-weary view of the world. The tango composer Armando Discépolo (1887-1971), for example, insisted that "tango is a sadness you can dance to", and added that for him, "life is an absurd wound". Discépolo took the sadness and regret of tango to existentialist extremes: *Yira Yira*, written in 1930 only a few months after the first military coup of the twentieth century, expresses all the pathos and bitterness of the frustrations of life in the chaotic twentieth-century metropolis. Together with *Mi Buenos Aires querido* and *Volver*, it soon became one of the most outstanding songs of Carlos Gardel's repertoire, and has been sung by every self-respecting tango singer over the past eighty years:

> *Veras que todo es mentira/Veras que nada es amor/que al mundo nada le importa/yira ... yira . . ./aunque te quiebre la vida/aunque te muerda un dolor/no esperes nunca una ayuda/ni una mano, ni un favor . . .*

> You'll see everything is a lie/You'll see that nothing is love/that the world couldn't give a damn/it keeps on spinning and spinning/even if you're broken by life/or eaten away by pain/don't ever hope for help/not a single hand, a single favour . . .

Like the *sainetes* of the turn of the century, and the later radio and TV soap operas, tango provides the inhabitants of Buenos Aires with their daily dose of melodrama, full of double-crosses, death and tragedy. In the end, the only person one can truly count on is the mother (the father often being absent, as in the case of Gardel himself). As the tango says: *Madre hay una sola* (We Have Only One Mother):

Besos y amores ... amistades ... bellas farsas,/y rosadas ilusiones, en el mundo hay montones/por desgracia/...Madre hay una sola! ...Y aunque un día lo olvidé/me enseño al final la vida/¡que a ese amor hay que volver!

Kisses and loves ... friendships ... all fine farces, rose-tinted illusions. In the world, unfortunately there is lots of this ... but we have only one Mother ... Although one day I forgot it, life in the end has taught me that we have to return to that love!

The 1940s witnessed increasing sophistication in tango music, and larger orchestras based on North American big bands. Following this trend, the vocalist was all-important, and often, as with Edmundo Rivero or Roberto Goyeneche, the more they sounded as though they had lived the tango life, the better. At the same time, however, Peronism's promotion of tango for political purposes as a part of a nationalist cultural heritage drove the conservative middle classes at least away from it. One of the most popular and important tango orchestras in these years was led by Aníbal Troilo; with him, lyrics writers such as Homero Manzi still managed to produce poetry based on nostalgia for the now disappearing world of the poor *barrios*, as in his famous *Sur*:

San Juan y Boedo antiguo, cielo perdido,
Pompeya y al llegar al terraplén,
tus veinte años temblando de cariño
bajo el beso que entonces te robé.
Nostalgias de las cosas que han pasado,
arena que la vida se llevó

pesadumbre de barrios que han cambiado
y amargura del sueño que murió.

San Juan and ancient Boedo, lost heaven,
Pompeya and the railway embankment,
Twenty-year old you trembling with emotion
From the kiss I stole from you.
Nostalgia for the things of yesterday
Sand that life has trickled away
Sadness of the changed neighbourhoods
Bitterness of the dream that died.

By now arguments broke out over what was "pure" tango, represented by the *guardia vieja* (old guard), contrasted with new, more experimental forms that drew inspiration from jazz or even classical music outside Argentina. These disputes coalesced around the figure of Astor Piazzolla (1921-92). A genius of the bandoneon, he met Gardel as a young boy growing up in Manhattan, and played with Aníbal Troilo in the 1940s, but left Argentina again to study composition, seeking to renew and purify the music of tango. From his *Adios Nonino* of 1959 (in honour of his dead father) to the score he wrote for the film *El exilio de Gardel* in 1985, he brought fresh ideas and a renewed intensity to the music. The old guard saw this as betraying the tradition, especially as Piazzolla's works were much more to be listened to than danced or sung, and rejected him as "too intellectual". But as in earlier times, the fact that his music became immensely popular and respected in the united States and Europe gradually won over tango lovers in his own city and country.

Meanwhile, by the 1960s the younger generations in Buenos Aires were more interested in rock music and music as protest than in the tunes their parents and grandparents played. Few wanted to listen to tango, and even fewer to dance it. As the political panorama darkened, it was the music of the Beatles and other rock groups that teenagers in Buenos Aires wanted to hear: the passion and sense of rebellion to be found there seemed far more real than the tired old stereotypes of tango. Somehow, though, tango survived even the bleak years of the military dictatorship. Many of the best singers and composers left Argentina for exile, among them the pre-eminent female tango singer of the 1960s and 70s, Susana Rinaldi, who headed for France. Once again, Paris became a centre for the best tango music and lyrics, with locales such as Les Trottoirs de Buenos Aires, which opened in 1981, keeping the flame alive. Then, as had happened many decades earlier, in the 1990s the music returned triumphantly to the Río de la Plata to engage a new generation.

Nowadays, thanks in part to the growth of tourism in Buenos Aires, tango can be found everywhere. As well as radio stations devoted entirely to the music, there are tourist cabarets which put on slick shows, world tango championships are held annually in Buenos Aires, there is a thriving gay tango scene and new, electronic tangos for young *tangueros*. Some of the old tango shrines still exist, such as the hundred-year-old and splendidly-named Confitería Ideal, situated only a few yards from Avenida Corrientes. There, almost every afternoon, a bizarre assortment of dancers get together to parade round the bumpy parquet dance floor, and sip beverages from tableware that itself offers a nostalgic journey into the past. At night, a hardcore of tango lovers, confusingly known as *milongueros* after the slow waltzes that often intersperse tango pieces, devote their lives to the *milonga*. This involves going out in the early hours to places where "authentic" tango music is playing: places like the Salon Canning on the street of the same name (although in 1974 a nationalist Peronist government changed the street to Calle Scalabrini Ortiz), which look unprepossessing from the outside and on the inside are all decrepit glory, with tables scattered round the all-important dance floor.

The protocols of finding a partner are often labyrinthine. The men walk round the dance floor, but rather than speaking to any woman they would like to dance with, communication is through a raised eyebrow, a nod of the head, a movement of the hips. On the dance floor, Buenos Aires tango experts disdainfully tell newcomers that it takes ten years just to learn the *caminar* or walk that leads couples into the dance proper. Perhaps this is why the best male tango dancers seem to have stepped out of the pages of 1940s films: slicked-back hair, pencil moustaches, a look of having lost everything that afternoon on the *burros* at the *hipódromo*. Although the tango is often seen as the macho dance *par excellence*, with the man choosing his partner and taking the lead in the steps of the dance, according to Argentine sociologist Marta Savigliano, tango offered many ways for the female half of the couple to assert herself as well:

> Milonguitas could challenge their male partners with the thrust and energy invested in the walks; manipulate their axis of balance by changing the distance between the bodies, the points of contact, and the strength of the embrace; play with diverse qualities of groundedness in their steps; modify the "front" given to their partners, choosing to "face" them in misaligned angles of torso and hips; disrupt the cadence sought by their partners by not converting their trampling *cortes* at the proper musical time (thus imposing a need for skilful syncopation in order to keep up with the music); and add unexpectedly fancy ornamentations or *adornos* of the figures "marked" by their partners.

The tango dance, then, is a passionate challenge, acted out during the twelve or so minutes that a *tanda* or group of tunes played together takes before there is a break in the music. In her book *Twelve Minutes of Love* the Bulgarian writer and tango *apasionada* Kapka Kassabova offers a local Buenos Aires psychoanalyst's explanation for the dance's fascination for both sexes:

1. Seduction (he invites, she accepts);
2. Engagement (they dance, they are together);
3. Rejection (they separate after a couple of tandas, thank you for the dance);
4. Fall (we were so close, and now we're strangers, I can't stand it);
5. Longing (please, I want to do it again).

8 | Leisure and Pleasure
Pastimes and Popular Culture

I t all started with the cattle and horses brought by Pedro de Mendoza and then by the second group of settlers who accompanied Juan de Garay in 1580. Many of the original stock escaped and found conditions on the pampas surrounding the new colony ideal in order to thrive and breed. The few dozen original animals became hundreds, then thousands, escaping to roam freely on the plains. The indigenous tribes, who had never known horses before, soon became expert riders, often swooping on the settlers in raiding parties or *malones* that became part of the colony's folklore. Equally skilled at horse-riding were the mixed-race *gauchos*, who trained horses and mules and slaughtered the cattle for their hides, leather and tallow fat, as well as for food.

It was not until well into the second half of the nineteenth century that the roaming herds of horses and cattle began to be contained in the huge ranches or *estancias* where the great wealth of Argentina was produced. Many *estancieros* or landowners had spacious country homes in a huge variety of styles, from mock-Tudor to miniature Versailles palaces, built several hundred kilometres from the capital, while at the same time owning luxury apartments or mansions as close as possible to the centre of Buenos Aires. As the livestock were not farmed intensively, but largely left to their own devices, for much of the year the ranchers did not need to be in what was known as *el campo* (or the camp, as it was known to the Anglo-Argentines). Instead they could enjoy the best of both worlds, with culture and sophistication in the capital, and simpler pursuits in the countryside during the scorching summer months, when according to a visiting Spanish writer, "it becomes too hot to think" in Buenos Aires. The rail network conveniently linked *el campo* to the city, while the richer landowners used their private planes. For the past four hundred years, this vast hinterland full of riches has underpinned everyday life in Argentina and Buenos Aires.

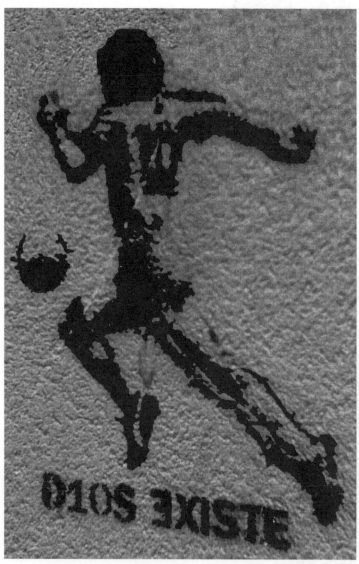

"God exists": graffiti tribute to the iconic Diego Maradona
(Antonio/Wikimedia Commons)

The agricultural produce from the hinterland has meant that unlike the less productive Latin American countries in the Andes or Central America, there have only rarely been food shortages for even the poorest people in Argentina. What most shocked many inhabitants of Buenos Aires during the economic chaos of 2001-02 was the sight on their TV screens of city shantytown dwellers desperately rummaging for food: something that was thought impossible in a country that enjoys the cornucopia of the pampas.

Naturally enough, this landowning class has supported values very different from those of the working classes and more progressive liberals in the cities, and in particular in Buenos Aires. General Perón and his followers made talk of the "oligarchy" a commonplace as a definition for his political enemies. As recently as 2008 and 2009, President Cristina Fernández de Kirchner employed very similar language in her attacks against *el campo* when her government wanted to hike the tax take on agricultural exports, a move that was resisted by the powerful landowners. For several weeks, landowners preferred to burn their crops rather than to submit to the new measures, and the city of Buenos Aires was covered day after day in thick, choking smoke and smog.

Apart from instances such as this, the presence of the world of the pampas in the city is nowadays usually more benign. In the north of Buenos Aires near Plaza Italia stand the grounds of the Sociedad Rural Argentina, known commonly as La Rural. Here once a year, the country comes to town in a show of the top breeds of cattle, sheep, horses and all the latest farming equipment, while the streets all around the Palermo site are clogged with the biggest and best 4x4s money can buy. The Sociedad Rural is in fact one of the oldest institutions in Argentina, set up in 1866 with the aim of "promoting improvements, progress and order with more effective grazing methods than those currently used, and combining these with tilling practices, studying livestock species and stimulating the welfare and morality of farmers". It now boasts some 10,000 full members, and as the recent spats with central government have once again demonstrated, can come together in a powerful union of interests.

The history over the past few years of the site of La Rural is also indicative of the country's history. The land on which it is built was public property until the mid-1990s, when President Carlos Menem, intent on selling off anything and everything that belonged to the state, sold the property to the Sociedad Rural. In turn, in 2005 a powerful banker purchased the land from the Sociedad, and quickly put it in the hands of a private company for a period of twenty-one years.

The only other occasion when Argentina's country heritage makes any direct impact on life in the capital is the "Day of Tradition" on 10 November each year. This date commemorates the 1834 birth of José Hernández, the author of the *gaucho* epic *Martín Fierro*, one of Argentina's foundational texts. Every year there are processions of riders in the Rural and other neighbourhoods of the capital. In 1996 President Menem also tried to create a Day of the Gaucho on 6 December each year, but this idea does not seem to have caught on.

The typical breed of Argentine pony ridden by the *gauchos* and farmhands has evolved over the centuries into a swift, sturdy animal. This makes it ideally suited to the two sports played on horseback in Buenos Aires. The more bizarre of the two is a game known as *pato*, literally meaning a duck. This is because in the colony's early days of the city, the opposing teams of horsemen would fight over possession of a live duck which had to be carried or thrown into the opposition's net. The poor animals rarely survived, and the sport itself was extremely brutal, as can be seen from this description: "It first set foot in Argentina almost four hundred years ago and the ancient game's practices consisted of throwing a duck upwards and two teams of horse riders got trampled underfoot while fighting to grab the duck and place it in a net." By the early seventeenth century, the game had become slightly more civilized (though still tough on the duck) according to a report by the historian Félix de Azara, who described a *pato* game in the city: "Two teams of men on horseback get together and two far away destinations are indicated. Later on, they sew the leather where a live duck sticking its head out has been placed. This leather is made up of two or more handles from which the two strongest men in each team hold on to half way between the destinations that have been signalled. Enthusiastically, they pull strongly until the strongest team grabs the duck and carries it with them, thus making their rival fall down onto the floor if they do not let the duck go. The winning team starts running and the opponents race after them and surround them until reaching them through one of the handles. They pull strongly once again, and the team that manages to carry the duck to the stated destination wins."

As with bullfighting, the game of *pato* was regarded as an un-welcome reminder of backwards Spanish colonial ways, and it was banned by the city authorities when Argentina won its independence early in the nineteenth century. According to an 1822 decree: "the punishment for anyone playing this game for the first time will be one month's hard labor and such penalty will be doubled if they are caught playing *pato* for a second time. Moreover, those caught playing *pato* for a third time will have to face a six-month hard labour period and shall be subject to redress the damage they may cause."

With the twentieth-century revival of interest in "tradition", a modern form of the game—using a leather ball with six handles on it, but without the duck—was introduced. Rules for the sport were laid down in 1934. It was in this same spirit of cultivating what was seen as "authentically Argentine" that in 1953 President Perón issued Decree Law No. 17,468 declaring *pato* to be Argentina's "national sport". Since then there have been yearly championships played at La Rural or on Buenos Aires' polo ground nearby in the north of the city, while the small town of General Las Heras in Buenos Aires province is the home of the Argentine Pato Federation.

While *pato* is regarded, even in Buenos Aires, as an oddity, the game of polo is widely seen as the ultimate expression of horseman-ship and skill, even though it is only played by a small number of the wealthiest Argentines. In common with many of Argentina's sporting pursuits, polo was first brought to Buenos Aires by the British: a former Indian army officer, David Shennan, is credited with having organized the earliest formal polo game in 1875. The sport quickly caught on, with the flat grasslands of the capital and the pampas providing ideal terrain for the skilful game. In 1892 the

River Plate Polo Association was founded, which a few years later became the Asociación Argentina de Polo. In the twentieth century Argentina became the global centre of the sport, with the country winning the competition in the 1924 Olympic Games in Paris, and again in Berlin in 1936 (the team's victory is still enshrined on the columns of the Olympic Stadium there, alongside all the German victors in the games). Nowadays championships are played at the Hurlingham Club or in the extensive ground in Palermo known as the "cathedral of polo".

If these two equine sports are largely enjoyed by wealthy Argentines, there are thousands of *burreros* who like to bet on the *burros* (donkeys) or horses at the Hipódromo, also located in Palermo. Once again, it was immigrants who organized the first "English races" in Barracas to the south of the city as early as 1826. It was not until 1876, however, when the Hipódromo Argentino was established in Belgrano, that horse-racing started to become a sport with a mass following. Since then, racing and betting have become part of the traditional Buenos Aires Sunday. The writer Ezequiel Martínez Estrada described its wide-ranging attraction in his *Radiografía de la pampa*:

> The South American hero is represented in the horse, and the gaucho wears a jacket of racing colours. The races are our bullfights, our tragic fiesta of blood, just as the football ground is our circus. The race-course attracts three different levels: the aristocratic, which in the *pur-sang* celebrates genealogical caste; the nationalist spirit, from the countryside in origin, with its worship of the horse, and the popular, which is part of our race, with its desire to challenge destiny in its betting.

Still part of the legends of *el turf* as it is known in Argentina are two races that took place as long ago as 1918. In the first, the undisputed champion Botafogo (owned by one of the most patrician families of the time, the Alvears) was surprisingly defeated by a younger rival, Grey Fox, in a field of four. Don Diego de Alvear could not accept the defeat, and challenged Grey Fox's owner to a return race just between their two horses a fortnight later. The entire population of Buenos Aires seemed to want to see the race: the Hipódromo gates were closed at ten in the morning, with 107,000 spectators already inside the stadium, although the race was only run at four in the afternoon. The newly emerging star of tango, Carlos Gardel, even absconded from a tour of the provinces to catch a train back to the capital to see the race. In the end, the chestnut Botafogo clearly showed his superiority, winning the second contest by some hundred metres.

Since then, the Hipódromo has witnessed many classic races, and numerous jockeys have risen to become the idols of the *burreros*. Perhaps the most famous of them all was Irineo Leguizamo, whose riding career stretched over five decades, during which time he won more than 3,500 races. When his friend Carlos Gardel became rich enough to own racehorses of his own, Legui as he was known rode his horse Lunático to nine consecutive victories in the mid-1930s. For lengthy periods in the twentieth century off-course betting on horse races was illegal, but predictably this only seemed to make it more attractive. In Buenos Aires, this kind of gambling was known as the *quiniela*, which also covered illegal lotteries and numbers games.

The Beautiful Game

Horses and the sports derived from them may be strong in Buenos Aires, and *pato* may have been officially declared Argentina's national sport, but for more than a hundred years, its sporting passion has been football. Like polo, it was brought to the Río de la Plata by the British, who promoted it in their schools and at their workplaces. Several of the city's local teams bear testimony to these origins, as with Ferro Carril Oeste (Western Railway) in the Caballito neighbourhood or Talleres (Railways Workshops) United Football Club, not to mention River Plate and Boca Juniors, the two greatest rivals in the city. As so often happened with sports originating in Britain, the newcomers to the game soon became as good, if not better, than their teachers. Argentina's national team has won the Football World Cup twice. Unfortunately, one of these wins was in 1978, under the military dictatorship, whose leaders used the occasion to show the progress they had brought to the country (this was when colour television first appeared on screens in Buenos Aires) and how they had restored national pride. The reality was much dirtier: the fact that Argentina was hosting the World Cup was without doubt one of the reasons why thousands of so-called "subversives" had to be dealt with quickly before the event was staged, and rumours persist to this day that the Peruvian national team was paid to lose to the hosts so that they could advance to the final.

Be that as it may, teams from Buenos Aires regularly win the Copa Libertadores de América, the South American club championships. Partly this is due to the clement weather, which allows the game to be played outside for most of the year. Perhaps it is also due to the mix of European immigrants who came to Argentina from Italy, Spain and other football-playing countries. The heyday of Argentine football was in the 1950s to 1970s, when players such as the legendary Alfredo di Stefano, born of Italian immigrants in the southern industrial district of Barracas, first went back to Europe to play in Spain and Italy, demonstrating how skilful Argentine players were. In the 1970s and 1980s came the phenomenon that was Diego Armando Maradona. Born in the poor southern suburb of Lanús, his rise from poverty to immense international success made him the idol of thousands of young Argentines. In Buenos Aires he played for both Argentino Juniors and Boca Juniors, before leaving for Barcelona and then Italy, where he helped Naples win the Italian football championship for the first and only time, as well as leading Argentina to victory over West Germany in the 1986 World Cup. Despite his erratic personal life after his retirement from the game in the early 1990s, Maradona is still revered by the vast majority of Argentines—there is even a church in his name, *la iglesia maradoniana*, promoted by his fans. Their version of the Lord's Prayer is:

Our Diego, who is on the pitches, Hallowed be thy left hand, bring us your magic. Make your goals remembered on earth as in heaven. Give us some magic every day, forgive the English, as we have forgiven the Neapolitan Mafia. Don't get caught offside and free us from Havelange and Pelé.

Since Maradona and his transfer to Naples, many of the best Argentine footballers have gone to Europe, where they can receive far higher wages than in Argentina. Lionel Messi at Barcelona is the latest of these highly successful exports. But losing the best players in this way, plus a lack of investment in the local clubs, has meant that football in Buenos Aires, even at the highest level, is in the doldrums. The endless repetition of games against the same opponents with little to distinguish them is frequently stultifying, although club loyalty is still immensely strong, and passed down from generation to generation. Furthermore, in recent years the phenomenon of hooligans, known as *barras bravas*, has led to unpleasant violence at matches. On several occasions deaths have been caused by brawling fans, leading to the suspension of competitions.

It is, though, an extraordinary event when the *superclásico* between Boca Juniors and River Plate takes place: 50,000 fans wave banners and hurl ticker tape on to the pitch while they shout themselves hoarse in the old-fasioned, open air stadium. And despite the falling-off of the professional teams, thousands of young *porteños* play the game intently, some hoping to escape poverty as their idols did, others just enjoying showing off their skills on an piece of waste ground in the city, in neighbourhood teams or indoors in breathless games of *futbol de salón* or *futsal*, the five-a-side variant popular throughout Buenos Aires.

Another sport imported in the nineteenth century from England which also has its enthusiastic, if more restrained supporters, is rugby. First played in English- speaking schools in 1873, it was enjoyed almost exclusively by British residents until 1899. For many years thereafter it was seen as an "upper-class" sport, although it did have some surprising participants, including the youthful Ernesto "Che" Guevara who played the game at school in Córdoba and then during his university studies in the capital in the late 1940s. Perhaps it was on the rugby field that he learnt the sense of "fair play" that subsequently led to him to his battles against imperialism in Cuba and elsewhere. In more recent times, as many as eighty rugby clubs have consolidated themselves in the more affluent northern neighbourhoods in greater Buenos Aires, such as

San Isidro and Olivos, and there is a well-supported national league, with almost 100,000 registered players. The national team, Los Pumas, usually comprising a majority from the Buenos Aires clubs, has long been a respected (and often feared) opponent in international competitions such as the Rugby World Cup. The strength of Argentina's rugby was recognized in 2012, when it joined the rugby giants of South Africa, Australia and New Zealand in a new annual southern hemisphere championship.

While rugby has grown in stature, the sport of boxing, which was hugely popular until the 1970s, has since gone into a relative decline. Earlier in the century Argentina produced a succession of heavyweights who challenged for the world title. We have already seen (in Chapter Three) how Luis Angel Firpo's defeat by Jack Dempsey rankled in the Argentine popular imagination—the outside world was widely seen as having cheated the country out of the international recognition that was its due. Growing up in the Buenos Aires suburb of Banfield, the young boy who became one of Argentina's most famous twentieth-century writers, Julio Cortázar, heard the fight relayed on his family's radio. According to him, this gave him a love of the sport that is not only reflected in several of his short stories, but even provided him with a metaphor for literary genres: "in the novel you win on points," he once declared. "In the short story, it has to be by knockout."

The tradition of rugged Argentine heavyweights continued into the 1960s and 1970s, typefied by figure of Oscar "Ringo" Bonavena. Born in Buenos Aires, he spent most of his life fighting in the United States. It was there in 1970 that he fought Muhammad Ali, and in what many Argentines see as a replay of the injustice committed on Firpo, he was knocked out by Ali in the last round, although the world champion is alleged not to have withdrawn as he should have done to a neutral corner of the ring, and therefore did not win "fair and square". Bonavena died in 1976 in a sordid shooting incident near Reno, Nevada. His body was brought back to Buenos Aires, where some 150,000 people filed past his coffin in Luna Park, once the temple to the "noble art" in the Argentine capital. He is buried near Firpo and Carlos Gardel in Chacarita cemetery, and a statue of him stands in Parque Patricios, near his birthplace.

An Art Deco extravaganza from the early 1930s, Luna Park was once known as the "palace of sports". Built near the riverfront in the heart of the city, the arena was also where Colonel Perón first met the then young actress Evita. Luna Park continues to put on boxing matches as well as basketball events, but is better known these days for its rock concerts.

Another sport followed with great interest in Buenos Aires and throughout Argentina is motor-racing. Like boxing and football, it has produced its national heroes, but in recent years has lost out because of economic and political difficulties. The most famous local driver was undoubtedly Juan Manuel Fangio. Born in Buenos Aires province of Italian immigrants, "el maestro" as he was known won the Formula One World Championship five times in the early 1950s, racing for four different teams. After his retirement he once again hit the headlines when in 1958 while on a visit to Havana he was captured by Fidel Castro's men as part of their campaign against the dictator Fulgencio Batista. Released unharmed two days later, Fangio remained friends with his captors although insisting "I never had anything to do with politics". Thanks to his influence and Perón's interest in the sport, an *autódromo* was built in the early 1950s on the outskirts of Buenos Aires. The Formula One World championship was held there on various occasions over the next 25 years, although it often fell foul of Argentina's chaotic economic and political situation; in 1982, for example, the race was suspended because of the Malvinas/Falklands War, while attempts to revive it in the late 1990s collapsed because of a lack of funds. Nowadays most of the motor-racing in Buenos Aires seems to be confined to drivers on its highways, who zoom in and out and overtake on all sides, perhaps to demonstrate their Italian heritage.

Food for Thought

Compared to their equine counterparts, the cattle which arrived with the Spaniards have not enjoyed such a varied and exciting destiny. Since early in the seventeenth century there are records of slaughter-yards or *mataderos* existing in the city. One of its districts is even called Mataderos, and there can be fewer sadder sights than that of the long line of trucks packed with animals waiting to be off-loaded into the pens in the yards, killed and butchered. At Liniers, several thousand head of cattle are dispatched every day.

Only after being butchered can cattle reclaim some of their glory. This is when their meat is grilled to make *asado*, another of the defining elements of Argentine culture. Out in the countryside, and in some city restaurants, whole sides of beef are cooked on a vertical spit over red-hot embers. More modestly, nearly all Argentine homes have their grill or *parrilla* where Sunday tradition dictates that several kilos of beef per person are cooked and consumed in a meal usually lasting several hours. Traditionally it is the man of the household who cooks the meat: the women lay the table, make the salads and orchestrate events in the background. A good *parrillada* is likely to start off with *chorizos*, spicy Italian-style sausages that are often served in a bun, making a *choripan*, the Buenos Aires equivalent of a hotdog. Also part of the first round are *morcilla*, or black pudding, and for those who can stomach them the *mollejas* (sweetbreads) and intestines or *chinchulines*, done to a crisp. Not much of the animal goes to waste, and that also applies to the main cuts that constitute the meal proper. There is *tira de asado* (spare ribs), *vacío* or *lomo*, the Argentine filet mignon. The beef is usually washed down with rough red wine, often cut in the peculiarly Argentine way with sparkling water from the soda siphon.

The British writer Gerald Durrell, in Argentina in the early 1960s collecting animals for his zoo, had this to say in *The Whispering Land* (1961) about the pleasures of an *asado* well-cooked in the open air: "to gulp a mouthful of soft, warm red wine, and then to lean forward and slice a fragrant chip of meat from the brown, bubbling carcass in front of you, dunk it in the fierce sauce of vinegar, garlic, and red pepper, and then stuff it, nut-sweet and juicy, into your mouth, seemed one of the most satisfying actions of my life." The sauce Durrell is referring to is *chimichurri*, almost the only accompaniment to the feast of meat-eating at an *asado*.

After such a blow-out there is only one thing to do: take a well-earned siesta before watching football on television, while the restorative *mate* is passed round. This hot digestive drink is one of the traditions passed down to drinkers in Buenos Aires from the countryside, where *yerba mate* is cultivated in the northern provinces. *Mate* is drunk following a simple but strict ritual. The *yerba*, which consists of rough chunks of the plant's leaves and stalks, is placed inside a gourd or *mate* that can be anything from a simple hollowed-out gourd to an elaborate silver artefact. The water should not be allowed to boil, but is poured hot onto the leaves and then sucked up through a metal straw or *bombilla*. The server or *cebador* usually takes the first drink, to make sure everything is as it should be. Then he or she hands out the prepared gourd to the right, and it is passed round in this way from drinker to drinker, without any cleaning between sips. A simple *gracias* indicates the drinker has had enough. (More than 2,000 *mates* from all over the world are proudly displayed in the Museo del Mate in Tigre.)

Apart from *mate*, there are not many regional dishes which are common in Buenos Aires, except for the ubiquitous *empanada*, the meat-filled pasty that is to be found in many Latin American countries, and *locro*, a heavy pork, maize and bean stew. Instead, each of the immigrant communities has brought something of its own cuisine to the Argentine capital. Although the Munich restaurants that served typical German/Austrian food have now disappeared, there are still many German-style restaurants and bakeries. Other delicatessens serve *masas*, varieties of small, sweet pastries that often accompany *mate*-drinking at the weekend. The most typical sweet biscuit is the *alfajor*, eaten not only in the capital but throughout Argentina. Its filling is another product of the pampas: *dulce de leche*, often translated as "milk jam". This consists of milk boiled and condensed until it is a sweet, cloying paste that children eat by the spoonful and which accompanies many desserts. There are also many restaurants from the different regions of Spain, particularly the Basque country, although despite the proximity to the river and with the Atlantic not too far distant, *porteños* still seem to greatly prefer meat to fish.

It is Italian cuisine that dominates. Not only are there pizzerias on every corner of the city but there are many more upmarket restaurants serving fresh pasta and many Italian regional dishes. In recent years, quality has become as important as quantity, although the city is credited with the invention of *sorrentinos*, said to be the largest kind of filled pasta in the world. And Argentine red wines, which have benefitted greatly from modernization and new foreign investment in the past two decades, have come to replace imported vintages.

The Italian influence is also evident in the many elegant shops and shopping malls in Buenos Aires. Because of the country's agricultural resources goods from leather and wool are particularly well-made, and as it lies in the southern hemisphere, the latest European fashions appear right on time for each new season in Argentina. Style is extremely important for both *porteño* men and women: one of the strangest sights in the few winter days of July or August is to see the rich ladies of Barrio Norte or Palermo parading in furs that for all the rest of the year are kept in refrigerated bank vaults. Of course, style is only important if it is admired by others: *porteños* are among the most gregarious people in the world. Restaurants, bars and cafés throughout the city are usually filled until the early hours with the middle classes out enjoying themselves. Professional families will probably have a maid (*muchacha*) and possibly even a cook or a cleaner at home to look after the children, and so go out themselves in the evenings to meet friends, attend meetings and enjoy the night-life.

It is not unusual to find these same professionals also indulging in another essential component of everyday life in Buenos Aires: psychotherapy. The Argentine capital, possibly because of its large Jewish population, is said to be second only to New York in the number of psychoanalysts and therapists of every stripe to be found there, especially in the better-off neighbourhoods such as Barrio Norte, Palermo or Belgrano. (Many immigrant Buenos Aires Jewish families dreamed of their sons becoming doctors, their daughter psychotherapists.) In the early part of the twentieth century mental therapy was regarded almost as a magical art—one of the earliest practitioners in fact "performed" cures in the capital's theatres, while another invented what he termed "psycho-enervation" and a third practised "natural psycho-analysis" in the woods around his hospital. As with so much else in Buenos Aires, it was immigrants from Europe who set the new discoveries on a more scientific and professional basis. One of these was the Swiss-born Enrique Pichon-Rivière, who made the Borda hospital in the suburbs of Buenos Aires famous for its analytical approaches to mental illness. The other, who joined Pichon-Rivière in setting up the influential Argentine Psycho-analytical Association, was the Jewish refugee from Vienna, Marie Langer (1910-87).

Through the 1940s and 1950s, she and other pioneers of psychoanalysis gradually increased their influence and the number of patients they treated. However, the psychoanalytical guru of the 1960s in Buenos Aires was the Frenchman Jacques Lacan. Possibly because he came from Paris, or because he was seen as a progressive, left-wing figure, his teachings enjoyed an extraordinary vogue among analysts and therapists, especially thanks to the efforts of the influential local analyst Oscar Masotta. In 1974, facing death threats, Marie Langer left Buenos Aires for Mexico, reputedly with only two hundred dollars in her pocket. Thanks to her and other *porteño* colleagues, the Argentine school of psychotherapy took root in places as distant as Mexico and Venezuela, while Langer herself went on to Managua in Nicaragua in order to help run therapy under the revolutionary Sandinista government.

Needless to say, this left-leaning, Jewish-connected pursuit was anathema to the military rulers after 1976. Analysts and therapists were persecuted, and a new wave set off into exile, taking their practices, for example, to Spain, just emerging from the long years of Franco's dictatorship and open to fresh ideas that had long been silenced by the previous regime. After the mid-1980s and the return of democratically elected governments, many of these therapists returned to Buenos Aires, where their trade continues to enjoy great success and prestige, even if nowadays shorter, less expensive and more dynamic forms of the "talking cure" have taken root. Throughout Latin America, Argentines and *porteños* in particular are known both for their love of analysis and their high self-regard, so that a common joke is: 'What's a *porteño*? The portable id we all carry inside us."

Newly arrived immigrants on a horse-drawn wagon, c.1900
(Library of Congress, Washington DC)

9 | Changing Faces
Migration and Social Change

By the time Argentina won its independence from Spain two hundred years ago, the population of Buenos Aires consisted of four main strands: the people who could claim direct links to Spain; those with distant links to Spain but mixed with indigenous ancestry; the indigenous population; and black people brought in as slaves and servants. Since then, the faces on the streets of the capital have changed dramatically. One of the city's demographic mysteries is the complete disappearance of its black population, making it very different from across the water in Montevideo or further north in Brazil. The other determining difference from elsewhere in Latin America has been the huge influx of European immigrants who have flocked to Buenos Aires from everywhere from Italy to the Ukraine. This mass migration has helped make Buenos Aires a "European" city, very different in atmosphere from say Lima, La Paz or Mexico City.

In the early twentieth century, almost half of the capital's inhabitants were either first- or second-generation Italian. Buenos Aires was also the world's third largest Spanish city after Madrid and Barcelona. There were additionally almost half a million people of Jewish descent, while until recently the German and British communities still had a very distinct identity. With increasing industrialization in the second half of the century, Buenos Aires witnessed an influx of darker-haired and darker-skinned people from the interior of Argentina as well as from poorer neighbouring countries such as Bolivia or Paraguay. There is still a social distinction between lighter-skinned "Europeans" and these *cabecitas negras* ("little black heads" as they are often demeaningly called), who are more likely to be employed in construction, or as maids and in other menial jobs.

According to the 2010 Bicentenary census, there are 2.9 million people living within the boundaries of the federal capital, and

15.6 million in the province of Buenos Aires, out of a total Argentine population of just over 40 million. Nowadays it is hard to believe that this huge city began with only some sixty settlers more than four centuries ago. Among the founding group who came down the river from Asunción de Paraguay, some were born in Spain or *peninsulares*, while others were already known as *criollos*, those born in the Americas. This pattern continued for much of the colonial period, with Spanish soldiers, administrators and merchants flocking to the southern outpost of the empire and intermarrying with the local-born Spanish-speakers. There seems to have been little mixing with the indigenous population in the city, however, although this was far more common in other areas of colonial Argentina. An interesting image of the pretentions of the Spanish colonial rulers is given in no less a book than Voltaire's *Candide*, written in 1759. Candide and his beloved Cunégonde have to flee Portugal on board a ship:

> They landed at Buenos Aires. Cunégonde, Captain Candide and the old woman called on the governor, Don Fernando de Ibaraa, y Figueora, y Mascarenes, y Lampurdos, y Suza. This great lord had the pride befitting a man who bore so many names. He spoke to people with the noblest disdain; he carried his nose so high, raised his voice so mercilessly, adopted such an imposing tone, and affected such a haughty bearing, that everyone who greeted him was tempted to hit him. He had a furious lust for women.

Women did indeed form part of the first expedition to set up the colony: according to a letter sent back from Isabel de Guevara to Princess Juana in Madrid, attacks by indigenous warriors and lack of food soon meant that "the men were so weak from hunger that it was the women who had to do all the work, washing their clothes, curing their wounds, cooking what little food there was, cleaning them, doing sentry duty ..." Several women came down from Asunción de Paraguay in 1580 for the second, successful foundation of the city. We know from Juan de Garay's records that one of them, Ana Díaz, was granted land in the colonial city he planned. More partners for the men of the colony were soon brought over from

Spain, but the imbalance between the two sexes became a feature of life that lasted well into the twentieth century.

While this relatively homogeneous white population grew steadily through the generations leading up to independence, the eighteenth century, and in particular the second half, was a period in which large numbers of black slaves arrived. Records show, for example, that between 1715 and 1739 British slave ships brought as many as 18,400 slaves from the coast of Guinea. Although many of these forced immigrants were sent to the provinces to work on plantations, those kept in Buenos Aires were employed mostly as manual labourers or as household servants. In 1744 a census estimated that one in every six inhabitants of Buenos Aires was black or mulatto: forty years later, this proportion had increased to one in four. On the eve of independence, there were almost 9,000 blacks and mulattos in the city. Over the following decade, their number increased to more than 14,000, only for this sector of the population to fall into a steep decline soon afterwards. By the end of the nineteenth century blacks and mulattos had become a rarity on the streets of the capital, and this is still the case today.

Many theories have been advanced for this dramatic disappearance. Black slaves were incorporated into the armies fighting for independence, and many fell in battle, while others chose not to return. After 1813 children born to slaves were considered free citizens with the result that the rate of intermarrying with the white population grew, but many of the freed population also appear to have chosen to cross over to Montevideo, where there was a larger black population already, or to travel still further north to Brazil. The blacks living in the poorer central neighbourhoods of Buenos Aires such as Monserrat, where many inhabited what was known as the Barrio del Tambor (the Drum District) were also more likely to be victims of the many epidemics that raged in the nineteenth century, especially the devastating outbreak of yellow fever in 1871. There is also little doubt that the immigration policies adopted by Argentine governments from Sarmiento onwards favoured white people from Europe, in a deliberate attempt to "improve the race". President Juan Alberdi, who in the 1850s coined the phrase "to govern is to populate", demonstrated this kind of racism when he declared: "who would not a thousand times rather have his sister or daughter marry an English cobbler than an Araucanian chieftain? In America all that is not European is barbaric." This view was endorsed by President Sarmiento, during whose term in office (1868-74) mass immigration from Europe became a flood. He spoke of the "Creole rabble, inept, uncivil, and coarse, that stops our attempt to civilize the nation", and was determined to see Argentina populated by educated German, English and French people.

In the following eighty years or so this goal was only partially achieved, yet there is no doubt that Buenos Aires is far more European in appearance than any other city in Latin America, and is also very dissimilar in atmosphere from the smaller cities of Argentina's interior. The few black people in Buenos Aires today tend to be Africans who have arrived in the city as refugees from violence in their own countries in recent years. These communities have moved into the less salubrious districts such as Barrio del Once, previously inhabited by poor immigrants from other countries.

Between 1840 and 1930 Argentina received 6.5 million immigrants from Europe. This meant it was second only to the United States as a destination, with more new people arriving in the far south of America than went to Canada (5 million) or Australia (3.4 million). In Spanish America, only Cuba could compare, but most of the immigrants there were from Spain, and this source of incomers dried up after the island won its independence at the very end of the nineteenth century. The influx to Buenos Aires began in earnest during the 1880s, with 841,000 European immigrants coming in through the port. As a result, the population of Argentina almost doubled in ten years. The figure fell somewhat during the next decade, with a little under 650,000 arrivals, but in the first ten years of the twentieth century poverty in rural Italy and Spain, as well as pogroms further east in the Russian empire, meant that the numbers grew to well over a million. Similar numbers arrived between 1910 and 1920, while from 1921 to 1930 another 1.4 million people made the more than 7,000-mile journey from Europe to Argentina. A high proportion of these newcomers from rural areas in Europe had been promised land to work in their new homeland. When they arrived this often proved a false hope, with the result that most of them were forced back into the towns and cities—and Buenos Aires above all—in order to make a living and bring up their families. By 1910, well over fifty per cent of the capital's inhabitants were first-generation immigrants.

Italians and Spanish

Of these new arrivals, close to half came from Italy. Due to lack of opportunity in the Italian countryside and political upheavals following unification in the 1870s, many thousands, particularly single men who were agricultural labourers, made the long journey in search of a better future in Argentina. Many stayed because the climate, agriculture and the way of life were similar to those in their home country. These agricultural migrants were sometimes known as *golondrinas* or swallows because they came to work in Argentina during the summer months, then disappeared during the winter to return to their native villages in Italy. Gradually, many of them also brought out wives and families to the new country, and often they then migrated to the capital and other Argentine cities to work in shops or small family-run businesses and factories where they could raise their families with more educational opportunities.

In 1914 there were more than 300,000 Italian-born inhabitants in Buenos Aires, some twenty per cent of the total, as well as more than a million with Italian parents or grandparents. (Perhaps the two most famous of these are Juan Domingo Perón, born in Argentina in 1895 of a Sardinian grandfather, and the new pope chosen in March 2013, Pope Francis I, whose father was an Italian immigrant who worked on the railways.) The first immigrants from Italy came from the northern provinces, and in particular from around Genoa. It is the Genoese dialect which is at the root of the unique Buenos Aires slang called *lunfardo*, impenetrable not only to foreigners but to many Spanish-speakers as well, incorporating as it does words from regional Italian: *laburar* for to work, *manya*, (food), *mina* (girl) and many unique expressions that became popular thanks to tango songs from the 1920s to the 1940s. This influence has also given an Italian intonation to the Spanish spoken in the city.

After the First World War, immigration from Italy switched further south, with many arrivals coming from Cantabria or Sicily. As in Italy itself, these new arrivals tended to be looked down on by their northern compatriots, but were soon assimilated nonetheless. Following defeat in the Second World War and the difficult economic situation in the immediate post-war years, a further 400,000 Italians are calculated to have disembarked in Argentina. The majority of them once more chose to live in Buenos Aires and the other main cities. Even today, more than half the population of Buenos Aires are of Italian descent, and in the country as a whole more than half a million people are still Italian citizens. Over the past thirty years, due to political and economic turmoil in Argentina, there has in fact been a reverse migration, with many thousands of young Argentines of Italian descent who could claim an Italian passport travelling to Italy in search of work or a more settled political atmosphere. Perhaps due to the circumstances which brought them to Argentina in search of work, there has always been fluidity of movement between their new and old home countries, so that many Argentine Italians still spend several months each year back in Italy. The Italians in Buenos Aires have left their mark in many areas, from language to fashion and food: the city has a pizzeria on almost every corner, pasta restaurants abound and a traditional working-class dish at Sunday lunchtimes is gnocchi. Then, of course, there is the love of opera and, some would say, the way that Argentines drive around the capital as though it was a racetrack.

Although the huge numbers of new arrivals from Italy brought fundamental changes to the structure of society in Buenos Aires, a third of all the nineteenth- and twentieth-century immigrants from Europe continued to come from the old mother country, Spain. In earlier centuries, the Spaniards disembarking in Buenos Aires had mostly originated in the provinces of the central plateau such as Castile and León. At the end of the nineteenth century these immigrants were replaced by newcomers from the northern coastal areas. Indeed, half of the new arrivals from Spain came from the north-western province of Galicia, where rapid population growth in the countryside had led to mass unemployment. Further considerable numbers arrived from the Basque country, and Catalonia. In the twentieth century, the presence of Galicians or *gallegos*, many of them speaking their own language, was so common in Buenos Aires that *gallego* has been adopted as a term (sometimes disparagingly, but more often simply affectionately) for Spanish immigrants in general.

In the single year of 1910, some 130,000 Spanish immigrants reached Argentina. Most of them stayed in Buenos Aires. Although the new generations of immigrants often had a complicated relationship with the traditional pre-independence families and the *criollos*, in the 1920s and 1930s there was a period of a national return to Hispanic roots which found expression in literature, architecture and the arts. During and after the Spanish Civil War, Buenos Aires became an important destination for many Republicans forced to leave Spain, and they set up clubs, restaurants and shops around Avenida de Mayo and in many of the city's neighbourhoods. During the forty years of Franco's rule in Spain, many of the texts censored there were published in Buenos Aires, and there was continued support for the Republic.

German-speakers

After the Italians and Spaniards, a third group of European immigrants who have contributed to the unique population mix of Argentina, and Buenos Aires in particular, are those who came from German-speaking countries. As well as Germany itself, many thousands made the voyage from Austria, Switzerland (as did the father of the recent president, Néstor Kirchner) and other territories in Eastern Europe. The earliest German-speaking immigrants founded agricultural *colonias*, but after 1870 many engineers and other specialized workers came and stayed in Buenos Aires. They set up their own schools, social clubs, restaurants and a newspaper, the *Argentinische Tageblatt*, which continued to publish daily news in German until the end of the twentieth century. As with the Italians and those from Spain, although the German-speakers came from very different backgrounds in Europe, once in Buenos Aires they tended to form a distinct community of their own. Many of them settled in the northern district of Belgrano, which still boasts many shops and restaurants with a German flavour.

It was during the crisis years after the First World War that the greatest number of immigrants arrived from Germany. In 1923 and 1924, for example, more than 10,000 came each year: half of them remained in the capital. There was a further surge following Hitler's rise to power in 1933, of whom many were German Jews. But there was a darker side to the German immigration as well. The Argentine army had been created on the Prussian model, and there was continued sympathy for Germany within the armed forces, as a counter-balance to British influence. The military governments in power in Argentina during the Second World War remained neutral before joining in on the side of the Allies in 1944, but they were notoriously more closely aligned ideologically to the Italian fascists and the Nazis. This was especially true of the then Colonel Perón. When he came to power in 1946, his government helped organize escape routes for Nazi and fascist officials in a scheme run by the Italian Catholic Church known as the Odessa network. Although Peronists prefer to downplay this aspect of Perón's rule, according to Jorge Camarasa in his book *Odessa al sur:* "Perón was closely involved in the arrival of war criminals into the country. In addition, he protected them, offered them homes and jobs, and even remained in contact with them in exile after his overthrow."

An estimated 5,000 Germans, Italians, Croats and others are said to have arrived in Argentina thanks to this escape network. For several months in 1945 it was even rumoured that Hitler himself had landed on the coast near the resort of Mar del Plata in a U-boat. Although this proved to be an unfounded rumour, many other unsavoury individuals did appear in the country. These included Hans-Ulrich Rudel, the leading Nazi fighter pilot, whom Perón encouraged to help create the modern Argentine air force. In the early 1950s Rudel proclaimed himself the "new Hitler" and returned to Germany to try to re-found the National Socialist Party. German scientists were brought in to establish Argentina's atomic industry on the outskirts of Buenos Aires. During the war, the Nazis had set up businesses and transferred large amounts of money to banks in Argentina, and so these new arrivals were well looked after. Perhaps the most notorious of these newcomers was Adolf Eichmann, one of the main organizers of the mass deportation of European Jews to the extermination camps. In 1960 he was seized near the rabbit farm he kept in greater Buenos Aires, and taken to stand trial in Israel, where he was eventually executed in 1962.

The Jewish City

This close relationship between the Argentine military, sectors of the Peronist movement and Nazi ideology has had serious repercussions for Argentina's Jewish population, the great majority of whom live in Buenos Aires. As well as accusing other Argentines of discrimination in employment and social relations, they have been the object of direct persecution. This was especially true during the military regimes between 1976 and 1983, when there is plentiful evidence that Jewish Argentines formed a high proportion of those abducted by the security forces, then to be tortured and "disappeared". Buenos Aires was also the scene of two bomb attacks in the 1990s. The first of these which killed 29 people at the Israeli Embassy in the busy centre of the city, the second causing 85 deaths with hundreds more wounded at the AMIA Jewish association in the central district of Once.

Such incidents and tensions have not prevented hundreds of thousands of people of Jewish origin from coming to Argentina, making Buenos Aires the city on the American continent (after New York) with the largest number of Jewish inhabitants (and also, as we have seen, second only to New York in the number of psychoanalysts and psychotherapists established there).

Some of the traders recorded in the early history of the capital were Portuguese Jews. Yet it was not until the second half of the nineteenth century that Jews began to arrive in much larger numbers, firstly from France and other Western European countries, and then increasingly fleeing poverty and pogroms in the Ukraine and Russia. (So many Jews arrived in Buenos Aires from Russia in these years that the common term for a Jewish person is still a *ruso*.)

Possibly the most ambitious immigration project was to try to create a "new Israel" in Santa Fe province, north of Buenos Aires. A certain Baron Hirsch had bought tracts of land there where the waves of Jewish immigrants could settle. The baron's idea was that for the first time since the biblical Israel they could work land that belonged to them. These were the famous *gauchos judios*, who reared cattle and sheep and adopted the lifestyle of the local *gauchos*. According to some writers, the fusion was complete: they began to eat barbecued beef (*asado*) without giving up their *gefilte fisch* and danced the local *malambo* with the same fervour as the polka. Within a generation, however, many of the new arrivals had deserted the land and found their way to the cities, especially the capital. They migrated especially to two neighbourhoods: the garment district of Barrio Once, close to the city centre, and the more suburban Villa Crespo (often commonly referred to as *Villa Creplach*). Both neighbourhoods had poor *conventillo* housing, tenement buildings with several patios where large families often shared a single room with few amenities, but they could also boast lively shops selling Jewish delicacies, theatres that put on productions in Yiddish until the 1940s, publishing houses (Jorge Luis Borges was first published by Manuel Gleizer, who fled a pogrom in Russia in 1908 and ended up in Villa Crespo) and clubs where the first trade unions and anarchist groups were formed, as well as the traditionally Jewish football club, Atlanta. Some verses by Israel Zeitlin, who also came to Buenos Aires at the age of one in the first decade of the twentieth century encapsulate this sense of dual identity:

I was born in Dniepopetrovsk,
the hazards of fortune
simply pass me by.
Argentine until I die
I was born in Dniepopetrovsk.

In the 1920s and 1930s, more Sephardic Jews began to arrive in Buenos Aires. They tended to congregate in the Flores neighbourhood, often taking over the houses of Italian immigrants who had prospered and moved further out of the city. Today, the Buenos Jewish population is some eighty per cent Ashkenazi, and most of them still have a strong sense of common identity despite being integrated into Argentine life. Their belief in the value of education has led to many second- and third-generation Jewish immigrants occupying important positions in the professions and the creative sector, as well as in business.

In the same years after the First World War, many thousands of immigrants came to Argentina from the Ottoman Empire. These newcomers tended to be called *turcos* or *sirio-libaneses* whether they were Jewish, Muslim or Christian, and whether or not they actually originally came from Syria or Lebanon. Immigrants from the Middle East often opened small corner shops, and their families spread throughout the country, although many remained in the capital. Recent estimates for the whole of Argentina put the number of people of Arab origin at more than three million; as with their Jewish counterparts, they have largely become assimilated into the population as a whole.

Many new arrivals from disparate backgrounds, cultures and traditions were flung together in the *conventillos* housing many families from different countries in one or two rooms. Adriano Bergero quotes a report on one tenement building and its occupants at the turn of the twentieth century in the newspaper *La Prensa*: "It was occupied by 48 people. In room no. 4, measuring 15 feet by 18, slept a married couple, a girl 15 years of age, and six men. In room no. 5, 15 feet by 15, slept a woman whose husband was in a hospital for infectious diseases, and six other men. Two kitchens sheltered 11 men, and room no. 7 had six more." While such living conditions often led to strife between the different immigrant groups, the remarkable thing seems to have been the lack of any widespread rioting or racial disturbances throughout this period of mass migration to the city one writer called "the new Babylon". Undoubtedly the insistence since the nineteenth century on system in which religious teaching was banned helped a great deal in lessening friction: whatever their origins, the new arrivals were quickly taught that now they were Argentines. The promise of upward social mobility also helped: in the first third of the twentieth century at least, the children and grandchildren of immigrant parents could hope to move out of the *conventillos* and poverty.

The Anglo-Argentines

Another immigrant group that to some extent always stood apart from the rest are the "Anglo-Argentines", who despite the fact that more often than not they came from Scotland, Ireland or Wales are always known as *los ingleses*, or "the English". Among the first to arrive in the city were traders in black slaves. They set up an office in 1714 for the sale of their human cargoes from West Africa. During the colonial period, Spain attempted to keep a monopoly on trade with Buenos Aires, and so foreign merchants were not encouraged to set up business there. Even so, the British ran an increasingly lucrative contraband trade in manufactured goods, taking hides and other agricultural produce back to Europe, and some settled in the Argentine capital.

Although the episode is hardly known about or taught in Britain itself, there were also two invasion attempts by British forces in 1806 and 1807, after Spain had been invaded by Napoleon's armies and the empire was collapsing. These invasion attempts were repelled (see p. 56) but some of the British troops and officers were welcomed into local families and stayed on. An unofficial census from the eve of Argentine independence in 1810 put the number of registered British citizens in the city at a mere 126, but they already had a British Commercial Room and even a *barrio de los ingleses* near Plaza de Mayo. With the freeing of commerce after independence, the number of British residents grew considerably, particularly when Britain recognized the new nation in 1825 and a joint treaty was signed guaranteeing freedom of worship to the Protestant British in Argentina, as well as burial in their own cemeteries. The following year saw the publication of one of Buenos Aires' first newspapers, the *British Packet & Argentine News*, which gave news of the community in Argentina as well as shipping and stock market reports. (The newspaper ceased to exist in 1859, but in 1876 the *Buenos Aires Herald* was launched, and is still published daily in English and Spanish.)

By 1830 there were some 4,000 British citizens registered in Buenos Aires (out of a total of about 70,000). The young Charles Darwin commented on what he found during a lengthy stay in Buenos Aires and Argentina in 1835, and his views remained typical of that of many British inhabitants in both the nineteenth and twentieth centuries:

> Sensuality, mockery of all religion, and the grossest corruption, are far from uncommon. Nearly every public officer can be bribed. The head man in the post-office sold forged government franks. The governor and prime minister openly combined to plunder the state. Justice, where gold came into play, was hardly expected by any one. I knew an Englishman, who went to the Chief Justice (he told me, that not then understanding the ways of the place, he trembled as he entered the room), and said, "Sir, I have come to offer you two hundred (paper) dollars (value about five pounds sterling) if you will arrest before a certain time a man who has cheated me. I know it is against the law, but my lawyer (naming him) recommended me to take this step." The Chief Justice smiled acquiescence, thanked him, and the man before night was safe in prison. With this entire want of principle in many of the leading men, with the country full of ill-paid turbulent officers, the people yet hope that a democratic form of government can succeed!

At the same time however Darwin did recognize many good qualities about the people he encountered in the city and country-side. Once again, his views may be seen to typify the more tolerant side of the Anglo-Argentine community:

> When speaking of these countries, the manner in which they have been brought up by their unnatural parent, Spain, should always be borne in mind. On the whole, perhaps, more credit is due for what has been done, than blame for that which may be deficient. It is impossible to doubt but that the extreme liberalism of these countries must ultimately lead to good results. The very general toleration of foreign religions, the regard paid to the means of education, the freedom of the press, the facilities offered to all foreigners, and especially, as I am bound to add, to everyone professing the humblest pretensions to science, should be recollected with gratitude by those who have visited Spanish South America.

As with other arrivals in Argentina, it was after 1850 that the number of British inhabitants of Buenos Aires increased significantly, although there was never a mass immigration akin to that of Italians and Spaniards. What chiefly drove the British presence was the fact that in the second half of the nineteenth century as much as eighty per cent of foreign capital in Argentina originated in the United Kingdom, and British people came out to fill the positions needed to control and administer this investment. British employees accordingly worked in banks, insurance and above all in the nascent railway and tram systems: almost forty per cent of the total British capital invested went on the growing railway network, built and run by British citizens. Since British people were employed by British firms with headquarters back in London, the community in Argentina frequently had little to do with the other immigrant groups, and as such the "English" remained aloof from the rest. This tendency was underlined by the creation of several schools where the sons and daughters of the immigrants were taught exclusively in English at private establishments run on the English model: St. Andrews, St. George's, Northlands and St. Hilda's continue to exist today. The English also set up members' clubs which were seen as the height of fashion, as well as helping to found the most powerful association of landowners based in Buenos Aires, the Sociedad Rural. And, of course, it was the English who brought many of the Victorian sports to Buenos Aires and Argentina. Football was first played in May 1868 on the grounds of the already existing Buenos Aires Cricket Cub in the Palermo district. A Scottish schoolmaster, Alexander Watson Hutton, is regarded as the "father of Argentine football" because in 1891 he set up the Argentine Association Football League, credited as the first one created outside the United Kingdom. But the English also brought tennis, golf, polo, rowing and rugby to the Río de la Plata, a fact which is still evident from many of the clubs' names.

The English also tended to congregate in specific neighbourhoods, usually at some distance from the city centre. Employees on the railways, banks and so on were to be found in the southern areas of Temperley or Quilmes. Those higher up the social scale headed north to Olivos or San Isidro (the home of today's best-known rugby clubs), while landowners often had a city base in Hurlingham, named after the club by the Thames in West London. The Buenos Aires version of the club was founded in 1888. It contains a golf course, a polo ground and even a cricket pitch, still used by homesick Anglos and visiting teams. A 1932 description by the writer Philip Guedalla precisely captures the spirit of Hurlingham: "Seventeen miles out of Buenos Aires, a charming suburb clusters around an admirable club. It has its games, its dances, and its life; and its contacts with Buenos Aires are almost confined to the successful effort of its male population to catch the morning train to town or lunch on Saturdays at Harrods."

The British influence in Argentina and Buenos Aires was so powerful that in his 1916 book *Imperialism: the Highest Form of Capitalism* none other than the Russian revolutionary Vladimir Ilyich Lenin speaks of Argentina being the most important unofficial colony of the British empire. This influence declined sharply after the Second World War, symbolized by the 1948 sale of the British-owned railways to Colonel Perón and the Argentine state. In the past fifty years, British capital and expatriate personnel have been almost entirely replaced by North Americans: they run the multinational enterprises housed in the gleaming steel skyscrapers down by the river, the international hotels, the English schools and even the English-language newspaper. In the most recent generations, the number of people still identifying themselves as "Anglos" has gone down from 70,000 to 15,000.

Recent Migration

In addition to North Americans, the main immigration currents of recent years have come from other countries on the same continent rather than from overseas. People from Bolivia, Paraguay or Uruguay have seen Argentina, and in particular Buenos Aires, as a place offering them greater economic and educational prospects. These newcomers, who often have manual labouring jobs in construction or industry, or who are employed as maids in middle-class households, also tend to be darker-skinned. This has led to outbreaks of xenophobia, particularly at times of economic hardship. In the late 1970s the military dictatorship passed the General Migration Act prohibiting undocumented immigrants from working and denying them access to public health care and education, while making it increasingly hard for them to legalize their situation. In 2003 the Mercosur governments passed an agreement allowing citizens to live freely in other countries of the customs union, but this has not prevented sporadic attacks on these newest arrivals.

Other newcomers who have suffered in this respect are the small community of South Koreans, many of whom run corner shops previously owned by Italian or Spanish immigrants in the poorer neighbourhoods. However, unlike cities such as Lima or Havana, until recently the Argentine capital had no real Chinese community. They were not brought in, as in those other countries, to work on sugar plantations or railways at the end of the nineteenth century (although the first recorded Chinese immigrant is said to have been employed by a British company running the Buenos Aires railway). Instead, their arrival has been much more recent. In the 1980s several thousand Taiwanese arrived, apparently fearing that their island would be taken over by the mainland communists. They have been joined in the past decade by people from Hong Kong and other southern coastal areas of China, and the latest estimates speak of some 100,000 Chinese who have settled in greater Buenos Aires or the surrounding province. The Belgrano neighbourhood now boasts a small "Chinatown" where Asian produce is sold and Chinese festivals are celebrated.

As has already been noted, from early on the Argentine state established a clear separation between religion and education. Before the 1810 revolution, it was the Jesuits who were in charge of education in Buenos Aires. They founded the Real Colegio de San Carlos in 1675, the forerunner of the Colegio de Buenos Aires, the most prestigious secondary school in the centre of the city. During the revolution, a pattern was established which has been repeated throughout the history of the Catholic Church in Argentina. Many of the ordinary clergy supported the struggle for independence, while the hierarchy was more conservative and opposed any change to the established order. Matters grew even tenser under the reformist government of Bernardo Rivadavia.

In 1822 he seized Church properties and abolished tithes and other privileges. These measures led to an armed revolt by devout Catholics, who succeeded in capturing the *cabildo* but were eventually defeated and their leaders hanged.

Tensions grew again between the state and the Catholic Church under the rule of Domingo Faustino Sarmiento. A freemason, he equated modern, progressive Argentina with freedom from religious beliefs: according to one story, he encouraged the spread of football on Sundays so that men would not go to Mass. Matters came to a head with the establishment of non-religious education in state schools in 1884. When the Catholic hierarchy opposed the move, students attacked churches and priests. Relations between the Argentine state and the Vatican were broken off between 1884 and 1899.

In the twentieth century the Catholic Church was once again split. On the one hand the Catholic workers' movement sought to defend the interests of the new immigrants. At the same time, the more conservative hierarchy sided with those trying to maintain order and restrain the social and political demands of the newcomers. When the military intervened in 1930, they were supported by the Catholic Church authorities, who continued to enjoy a close relationship with them through the rest of the decade and the war years. Conflict between Church and state flared up again during Perón's second government. Perón, especially after his wife Evita's death, regarded the Catholic Church as an enemy. On several occasions, Peronist mobs sacked churches in Buenos Aires. So it was that when Perón was ousted by the military in 1955, the Catholic Church once again backed the coup.

Even more controversial was the Church's silence during the repression that took place after the 1976 military takeover. The Catholic Church made no protest over the thousands of disappearances, and did little (unlike its counterpart in Chile) to offer help to the families of the "disappeared" in Buenos Aires or among those accused of staying silent in the face of the atrocities committed is the new pope, Francis I. As head of the Jesuit order in Argentina at the time, he is said to have done little to prevent the persecution of several priests from the order, as well as not speaking out in defence of human rights during the brutal military dictatorship.

This acquiescence greatly damaged the Church's reputation among ordinary people, and helped the surge in evangelical Christian churches that was evident in the 1990s.

Since independence, there has been freedom of worship in Buenos Aires, and many different religious communities have thrived. There are thousands of Hasidic Jews, Anglicans, German Protestants and Muslims. The most visible symbol of this religious freedom is the Russian Orthodox Church next to Parque Lezama. Its blue onion domes and gleaming white walls have made it into one of the city's icons ever since its construction in 1904. Designed in St. Petersburg on the orders of Czar Nicolas III, its first members were, in fact, Orthodox Christians from Greece and Yugoslavia. Their numbers grew with refugees from the Ottoman Empire, but nowadays only a few continue with their faith.

A much more recent icon is the huge mosque completed in the year 2000, close to Argentina's national polo ground in the north of the city. Known as the King Fahd Islamic Cultural Centre, it can hold up to 2,000 worshippers and is the largest mosque in Latin America.

Although many of these religions thrive in Buenos Aires, between eighty and ninety per cent of its inhabitants still classify themselves as Catholic. The disillusioned description of a "typical" Catholic given by the priest Leonardo Castellani in the 1950s may sum up the attitude to religion of many of these people:

> Is he a Catholic or not? He was baptised at seven months, has taken first communion, was married in Church (he paid the priest 50 pesos and let himself be led to the altar dressed up to the nines). And when he dies he will be taken to church again and sprinkled with holy water and mangled Latin. He knows little or nothing about religion. He goes to Mass whenever he feels like it. His head is stuffed with heretic or misguided ideas, put there by newspapers, magazines, and novels. He lives a very elastic and exterior morality ... His faith consists of a vague mythology that has little relation with real life. Is he a Catholic? If you want to call him so, that's your business, but I don't. Something similar is true of the Argentine nation. Taken together it's a cheap, shabby thing.

10 | Consuming Passions
Money and Shopping

For a short while in Buenos Aires in the 1970s I was a million-aire—once an hour. The Argentine *peso* was so devalued that this was what I could charge for my English lessons. Inflation was so rampant that, even though it never quite reached the stage of Weimar Germany with people pushing wheelbarrows full of notes, all transactions were strictly in cash and on the spot. No cheques were accepted, no deferred payments. On a long distance overnight bus to the resort of Mar del Plata, the driver suddenly stopped in the middle of nowhere and demanded that we all pay the full ticket price a second time: the price of fuel had doubled at midnight, and he needed funds to buy more petrol. With the *peso* becoming ever less valuable, there was a scramble to acquire US dollars. Shabby men on the corners of Calle Florida, with lookouts posted a few yards away, would hand over grubby-looking greenbacks in return for bags full of Argentine banknotes, giving clients little chance to check whether what they were getting was real or forged. Anything beyond everyday purchases of food, fuel and so on was carried out in the North American currency, creating a hysteria that involved everyone from the wealthiest to the poorest *mucama* or maid. These latter were often sent out to buy up as much as they could of house-hold goods before they too doubled or tripled in price: the price stickers on most items were changed every day.

The military rulers in March 1976 overthrew Isabel Perón's incompetent and corrupt government promised to return order not only to Argentina's political life, but to its economy as well. Although the measures they took in this area were not as murderous as in dealing with political opponents, they were extremely drastic. With Alfredo Martínez de Hoz, a member of one of Buenos Aires' richest land and property-owning families, in charge as minister of the economy, the first move was to knock six digits off the bank-notes. So instead of being a multi-millionaire, I was earning just one

The Stock Exchange or *bolsa*, scene of many crises
(Antonio Garcia/Wikimedia Commons)

peso an hour. Like everyone else, though, there was nothing I could do about it. Many trade unionists had been "disappeared" or imprisoned, businesses of all sizes found they had a military *interventor* controlling their financial affairs—and it was impossible to protest. The men on the street corners disappeared as if by magic, and for a while the currency stabilized. Now the fraudsters made their money by confusing foreigners and the unwary with the numbers of noughts in the new prices, and what the old notes were worth. There was nothing new in any of this, a veteran academic historian told me at the time: the economy of Buenos Aires has been following this cycle for the past four hundred years.

Export Economy

In the early days of the new colony, Buenos Aires struggled to assert itself as an Atlantic, European-facing port and as a small, insignificant part of the Spanish empire, whose main economic concerns lay elsewhere. From the start, Buenos Aires made its living from contraband or the colonial administration. There were strict regulations regarding trade with the French, Dutch or English, who were keen to buy and sell with the growing settlement. But the Spanish crown stipulated that all goods exported or imported had to pass through the vice-regal port of Callao in Peru, several thousand kilometres to the north, from where they were shipped to Panama, then sent overland again to Portobello on the Atlantic side of the isthmus, and from there to the imperial ports of Cádiz and Seville.

The temptation to find a way around these strictures was obvious, and in the seventeenth and eighteenth centuries a flourishing black market trade in silver from Potosí, *yerba mate*, timber and other products from the provinces upriver in northern Argentina, as well as hides and tallow from the pampas, brought these commodities to Buenos Aires and out of the country to Europe. The Spanish authorities in the estuary city tried to impose duties and taxes on trade both up towards Peru and out through the port of Buenos Aires, but the revenues raised in this way appear to have been largely spent on defence against the Portuguese and other foreign powers trying to gain control of the Río de la Plata region rather than on stimulating commerce. As correspondence of the time (quoted by Jonathan C. Brown) reveals: "deprived of European goods that they called 'necessities', residents [of Buenos Aires] complained that Lima's merchants infrequently sent cargoes to them overland. When European clothing, wine, oil, and weapons did arrive from Peru, their prices were prohibitive and the quality poor. Woolen cloth that cost two and a half pesos in Spain brought twenty pesos in Buenos Aires. Moreover, townspeople lamented having to export their hides and dried meat over the Andes, when direct shipments of native products to Brazil brought twice their original cost."

These strict rules were gradually relaxed, particularly with regard to the import of African slaves. In Buenos Aires, the Portuguese merchants unloaded their human cargo and illegally loaded flour, tallow and leather hides to take back to Europe. The Portuguese were the first foreign traders to set up business in the city, using the profits from the slave trade to import goods from Europe that they sold without permission both in the port and in the then larger cities in the north of Argentina. Dutch, French and British companies followed suit in the eighteenth century, taking on goods without permission in the port or further down the river. When the Spanish authorities gave the Río de la Plata more autonomy in 1776, there was a new boom in trade. With a population now of over 40,000, the "great village" itself was a growing market for goods, which in turn meant that a nascent merchant class began to prosper. Jonathan C. Brown has painted a picture of the trading class in the city at the start of the nineteenth century: "Numbering about 178, the import-export wholesalers, or *comerciantes*, conducted all trade from the port, controlled most capital resources, and arranged freighting of goods to interior markets . . . They invested in auxiliary economic activities, such as retail sales, coastal and river shipping, and meat-salting plants, but rarely in rural land.' Brown also calculates that there were around six hundred retailers of cloths and other imported goods early in the nineteenth century, while there were even more *pulperías* or general stores selling everything from imported spirits to candles, salt and other consumer goods.

These merchants were among the *porteños* keenest to throw off the last vestiges of Spanish restrictions over the local economy, so that Buenos Aires could trade freely with the rest of the world—above all, with the newly emerging industrial power of Britain. Following independence, the next generation of rich local business-men did begin to buy land and create large agricultural enterprises, and their products found a ready market in Britain. At the same time, machine-produced goods from Europe were increasingly seen as "necessities" by better-off inhabitants, while tools and machinery for the incipient local industries were also financed through capital raised on the London stock exchange.

Markets and Stores

Commerce continued to be dominated by small-scale outlets, most of them still concentrated around the old centre of the city—the Recova in Plaza de Mayo, and more prestigious stores on Calle Florida and nearby streets. It was not until 1880, when Buenos Aires was named the federal capital of the republic, that Mayor Marcelo T. de Alvear began significantly to remodel the city. Part of this "modernization" included the building of more hygienic indoor municipal markets where meat, fruit, vegetables and other fresh produce was sold. In keeping with contemporary tastes, they were based on European designs—in this case, Paris or the markets in large Spanish cities. They provided spacious and well-planned facilities that replaced the old, often ramshackle outlets of colonial times. These markets and small neighbourhood corner shops—butchers, fruiterers, bakers—are still the mainstay of daily shopping in Buenos Aires. Rarer these days are the itinerant merchants and hawkers who roamed the streets of the *barrios* for centuries, a variety of tradesmen that the Argentine-Canadian writer Alberto Manguel recalls with nostalgia from his childhood in the neighbourhood of Belgrano in the early 1960s:

> Along the cobblestones outside my house, the horse-drawn cart of the man who sold soda-water would rattle in the early morning to deliver the wooden crates stacked with half-a-dozen green or blue siphons that the cook stashed away in the laundry-room. The rag-and-bone man would come, pushing his wheelbarrow, looking for old clothes to buy, and the knife-sharpener, dragging along his whetstone on a curious wheeled contraption would blow on his harmonica to announce his passing. There was a chemist-shop at the corner that always smelt of eucalyptus, and down the other way, a stationery store that sold the most wonderful selection of notebooks and pens.

In the city centre, another import from Europe revolutionized smart shopping. In 1883 an Englishman by the name of Alfred Gath got together with the Spaniard Lorenzo Chaves to open the first department store. At first selling mostly English cloths for men, it quickly became fashionable and added a women's department. By 1901 Gath & Chaves had a four-storey building all to itself on the corner of Calle Florida, and was established as *the* place for *porteño* high society to buy all its imported goods, from suits and dresses to perfumes, toys or grand pianos. The store also boasted a factory making furniture, and elegant cafés and food departments. In 1914 a new "belle époque" building designed by the French architect Fleury Tronquoy offered seven floors of goods to its customers, creating one of the city's architectural landmarks of the early twentieth century. In its heyday, Gath &Chaves also had branches in Santiago de Chile and nineteen cities throughout Argentina. But the owners were unable to keep up with more modern shopping trends, and the group was forced to close in 1974. Its main headquarters on Florida and Calle Cangallo was converted into a bank.

Gath and Chaves helped found an even more iconic landmark in the city: the Harrods department store on Calle Florida, the only overseas branch of the famous London business. This venture also met with great success, to the extent that in 1920 it occupied almost an entire block, "crowned by an eight-storey cupola overlooking Córdoba Avenue, and featuring marble steps and cedar flooring throughout, as well as wrought-iron elevators with a riding capacity for twenty, valet service, and a jazz orchestra". Like Gath & Chaves, though, the Buenos Aires Harrods fell on hard times in the troubled 1970s and 1980s, and when Mohamed Al-Fayed bought the London business, there was lengthy legal wrangling over the Buenos Aires store's right to use the brand name. Harrods Buenos Aires closed at the end of 1999, only months before the economic crash of 2001. More recently, the Swiss venture capital firm that now owns the Harrods building has announced plans to return the store to its former glory.

Crash and Burn

The 2001 crash marked the end of a decade of *plata dulce* (money as sweet as the Río de la Plata had seemed to the original Spanish explorers). As Naomi Klein wrote in the London *Guardian*: "1990s

Buenos Aires went on a career and consumerism jag that would put the most shopaholic, workaholic New Yorker or Londoner to shame. According to government data, between 1993 and 1998, total household spending increased by $42 billion, while spending on imported goods doubled over the same high-rolling five years, from $15 billion in 1993 to $30 billion in 1998." With the *peso* so strong, middle-class families in Buenos Aires not only became conspicuous consumers, they travelled abroad to Europe, Miami, South Africa, and converted as much Argentine currency as they could into dollars, often depositing them in the new foreign-owned banks that also sprang up in the City in the final years of the millennium. Those *porteños* who saved in this way knew from bitter experience that this boom could not last. When the Radical Party's Fernando de la Rúa came to office as president at the end of 1999, he was faced with the consequences of a decade of high public and private spending, corruption, government deficits and the lack of any definite policies to remedy the situation.

By mid-2001 the economy was once again in ruins, and De la Rúa lost all remaining credibility when he re-appointed Menem's henchman Domingo Cavallo as economy minister. All those who could took their dollars out of Argentina, including many of the foreign investors. This proved to be a wise move, because in December 2001 Cavallo imposed tight restrictions on the amount of money anyone could withdraw from their bank accounts, and prohibited any US dollar withdrawals. This move, immediately known as the *corralito* (from the rounding up and penning of cattle) soon unleashed a popular fury that exploded on the streets of Buenos Aires. Foreign banks were attacked in La City, stores and supermarkets raided, roads blocked by protestors. By 2002 Argentina's GDP had fallen by some twenty per cent in four years, and unemployment had more than tripled to one quarter of the workforce.

The effects were instantly visible on the streets of the capital. For the first time, there were beggars on the street corners of fashionable areas such as Palermo or the Barrio Norte. Soup kitchens and food dole-outs became commonplace, as did the phenomenon of the *cartoneros*, described elsewhere in this book. Argentina, which had long argued it should not be seen as an exception in Latin America, came to resemble its neighbours in the most negative way—through poverty, unemployment, and even hunger, in one of the world's most fertile and productive countries.

The violence in the very centre of the city spelled a further decline of Calle Florida's reputation as the smartest area to shop in. It became taken over by stores selling cheap leather goods or tourist trinkets, while more discerning *porteño* consumers preferred to shop in the new malls rapidly being built. Some of these, such as the Patio Bullrich in Retiro, were created by remodelling old buildings. The Bullrich shopping centre stands on the site of the nineteenth-century auction house owned by the Bullrich family, where everything from livestock to family heirlooms were once sold. Completely overhauled in the late 1980s, it was the first of a new generation of malls that offer international fashion, fast-food outlets and restaurants, cinemas, cafés and other recreational possibilities. Similar make-overs have involved the complete renovation of the Galerías Pacifico (on Calle Florida) and the old fruit and vegetable market of Abasto, now said to be the largest mall in the city, with more than 230 shops and other attractions.

Buenos Aires has always been a trading city. At times it seems as though its entire population is busy buying and selling, from the smartest boutiques on Avenidas Callao or Alvear to recent corner stores run by Korean immigrants. There are huge shopping malls, streets in a neighbourhood like Barrio Once where tiny outlets specialize in everything for the garment trade, and weekend markets in parks and squares offering everything from hippy trinkets and leather goods to bric-a-brac and a few genuine antiques. In their country's chronically zigzagging economic climate, *porteños* have learnt to keep a sharp eye open for a bargain, and know that it is better to buy today than to save for an uncertain tomorrow.

11 | **The Dark Side**
Crime, Vice and Terror

A s both a port city and one close to a violent frontier, disorder and crime were pre-occupations for Buenos Aires' inhabitants from the earliest days. The countryside around and its outskirts, or *orillas*, where the pampas gave way to the first rough buildings were at first seen as the greatest threat to law and order. Here were the *pulperías* or low bars, the rudimentary brothels and the places where early tango and other types of music were played. As Richard Slatta and Karla Robinson describe them, "these cramped, primitive stores furnished a miscellany of general merchandise, food stuffs, and liquor sold to slaves, who shopped for their masters, and to lower-class patrons. Gamblers, inflamed with the pulpero's ready supply of cheap but potent liquor, often duelled with long, sword-like knives known as *facones*. Death or serious injury frequently resulted." And as a nineteenth-century Scottish traveller observed: "numberless are the crosses about the doors of the pulperías".

The criminal elements were known as the *orilleros* (men from the margins). They were the ones who brought the "uncivilized" ways of the *gauchos* and the native tribes into the growing city. Later writers such as Jorge Luis Borges romanticized the violence of *compadritos* or neighbourhood toughs keen to seek a fight and finish it with a knife thrust in the name of honour, but in the early nineteenth century they were regarded with suspicion and fear. In response to these fears, the first municipal police force was created in Buenos Aires in 1827. By 1837 this force had grown to some 60 mounted officers and 45 *peoneros de policía* who patrolled on foot. Their main concerns were the crimes committed by these vagrants, and public order disturbances.

As waves of European immigrants started to arrive during the last thirty years of the nineteenth century, so the emphasis on crime changed. Instead of danger invading the city from the wild pampas, now it was criminal elements among the newcomers who were seen

The Pirámide de Mayo covered with photos of the *desaparecidos*, the
"disappeared" victims of the military dictatorship in the 1970s and 1980s
(WikiLaurent/Wikimedia Commons)

as the greatest threat to public order, especially since a large proportion of the new inhabitants were young, single males. It soon became
a commonplace to view the southern European immigrants from
Italy and Spain as responsible for most violent acts. An Argentine
criminologist wrote in 1909: "more than 50 per cent of the criminals
of different nationalities, especially Spaniards and Italians, are alco-
holic degenerates, and many others are habitual drunkards." Recent
analysis of police records suggests, however, that proportionally the
most troublesome elements were the British (apparently because of
the large numbers of seamen coming ashore for short periods) or
labourers from neighbouring Uruguay. Other statistics show a different aspect of the dangers facing the Buenos Aires police: in the
thirty years between 1884 and 1914, as many as 50 of them were
killed in political attacks.

As Buenos Aires grew and modernized, the first National Penitentiary was built in 1877. A competition was held, won by local architect Ernesto Bunge. His design for a semi-circular prison with five wings was based on the "panoptic" construction (where the guards could see every cell, but the prisoners were kept entirely separate from each other except for work periods, and there was a rule of absolute silence) pioneered at Pentonville Prison in London. Situated in the north of the city on the upper-class Avenida Las Heras, the Buenos Aires penitentiary immediately became a landmark. It was regarded as a symbol of progress in the humane treatment of its inmates. Prisoners previously held in the central *cabildo* in Plaza Mayor were transferred to the 704 cells in the new, "enlightened" institution. Not everyone, however, saw isolation and silence as progress: in the second part of the great epic of gaucho life, *Martín Fierro* by José Hernández, the *gaucho* imprisoned there has this lament: *No es en grillos ni en cadenas/En lo que Usted penará/ Sino en una soledá/Que parece que en el mundo/Es el único que está* ("It's not in shackles or in chains/That you will suffer there/But in such solitude/It seems in all the world/You are the only one").

At first the new penitentiary stood on empty land, but in the course of the twentieth century it gradually became enveloped by apartment buildings as the city continued to grow. It was finally demolished in the early 1960s, to produce one of the few large green spaces in the heart of the city. (Recent figures show that Buenos Aires has only an average of 1.77 square metres of green space per inhabitant, whereas New York has twenty.)

However strict the regime in the National Penitentiary, it was far preferable to ordinary prison or being incarcerated in a police cell. In common with many other Latin American countries, no distinction was made in Buenos Aires between those prisoners who had been accused of an offence and were awaiting trial, and those who had been found guilty and sentenced. According to local criminologists, throughout the twentieth century more than half of all those held in prisons or police cells were at least technically innocent of any crime. Despite the huge rise in population, the government budget for prisons has always been minimal, and attempts to modernize the regime and conditions were frequently regarded with suspicion, especially during the long periods of military rule. The inherent slowness of judicial proceedings in the Argentine legal system based on the presentation of written statements, and the widespread corruption and politicization of the judiciary, only added to the prisoners' problems.

The "White Slave Trade"

The majority of the new immigrants arriving from Europe were young males, and the gap in numbers between men and women living in Buenos Aires widened accordingly. The Argentine sociologist Ernesto Goldar has calculated that in 1914, for example, sixty per cent of males in the city were foreign-born, and that there were some 600,000 more males than females between the ages of sixteen and sixty. These uprooted males often turned to prostitutes to satisfy their sexual (and frequently emotional) needs.

Prostitution and criminal elements had obviously existed in the pre-nineteenth-century city. These were mostly confined to the shacks and small farms in the south, where people from the pampas came in with their animals. The first municipal ordinance on prostitution dates from 1875, when brothels were legalized and taxed. This initiative, as Donna J. Guy points out in her study *Sex and Danger in Buenos Aires*, was aimed more at protecting society from the perceived threat to public order than out of any concern for the welfare of the women involved in the sex trade. As she writes: "At the end of the nineteenth century Buenos Aires had a terrible international reputation as the port of missing women, where kidnapped European virgins unwillingly sold their bodies and danced the tango." This white slave trade periodically caused outrage in Europe. As a correspondent wrote to an 1899 British National Vigilance Congress:

There are hundreds of wretched parents in Europe who do not know whether their daughters are alive or dead, for they have suddenly vanished ... Well, we can tell where they have been brought to and what has become of them. They are in Buenos Ayres or Rio de Janeiro ...

> This trade is a very lucrative one, for the men in South America are of a very amorous disposition, and "fair merchandise" from European lands easily finds buyers. If anyone wants to find out how the girls are treated they may simply take a walk along the Calle Juan and the Calle Lavalle, those two streets that have been nicknamed by the people "Calle Sangre y Lagrima" (The Streets of Tears and Blood).

Donna Guy's book challenges many of the assumptions of this "white slave trade", arguing that often the women were not as passive as this slogan suggests. What is not in dispute is that most of the prostitutes at the turn of the century were foreign-born (some 65 per cent of them according to 1903 statistics), and that many of them were Jewish from Eastern Europe. A Jewish procurer from Buenos Aires would travel out to the *stetl*, to find poor families where the girls were seen as a burden. They were promised a new life and husband over the ocean, and subsequently bought for a small sum, or paid to marry a young man. They would then be taken on the long boat journey across the Atlantic to Montevideo in Uruguay, and then by land or sea across into Argentina and down to Buenos Aires. Once in the city, the girls were sold at auction. The Café Parisien on the corner of Avenida Alvear and Billinghurst became particularly infamous in this respect. In 1932 the former police inspector Julio Alsogaray wrote of these auctions, where the girls were displayed naked:

> No sooner had the curtains been drawn back than the bidding began. Men and women would throw themselves on the poor victim, driven by a repugnant sense of greed. They would feel how firm the girl's flesh was, judge the overall appearance of her body and breasts, and in particular her teeth and hair. The goods were sold to the highest bidder, who paid at once in pounds sterling. The girl was then taken off to the brothel ... the purchasers often brought their wives with them, who were equally keen to examine the victim. Only very rarely did the price go above £45, when the woman on offer was exceptional. These auctions took place two or three days after the girls arrived, and took place three or four times a month.

This trade was frequently controlled by Argentine Jews. In 1906 they formed the so-called Warsaw Mutual Aid Society as a cover for their operations. This was later split into the Asquenasum and the Zwi Migdal. By the 1920s, this latter group was calculated by the police to have five thousand members who controlled two thousand brothels, where some thirty thousand women worked. Members of the Zwi Migdal dressed like rabbis and met in a fake synagogue on Calle Córdoba. The figure of the extravagant pimp soon passed into common folklore: in 1905 the writer Manuel Gálvez described a *caftén* in these terms: "The caftén loves ostentation. He dresses expensively—in brothel style—where everything is for show and vulgar. He has enormous rings on his left hand, and his cane is gold-topped. The drunken red of his necktie matches the red of his stockings; his silk handkerchief is too big and ridiculous-looking." The number of words for pimp also testifies to the impact they made on the popular imagination: as well as *caftén* (possibly because of the long coats worn by Orthodox Jews in Eastern Europe) they were known as *rufián, macro, lenon, cafishio, alcahuete, chulo, heweman, sicotaro, marlú, cafiolo, souteneur* and so on.

The most highly-prized among the foreign prostitutes were French women, or those who claimed to be from France. According to one writer, the *maquereaux* running many of the French prostitutes in Buenos Aires used to meet in the back-room of the French bookshop in the centre of the city, while in the front Catholic and devotional books were on display. The tales of how unwilling young Frenchwomen were hauled off to the distant south to be exploited as prostitutes led to one of the best-known books on the trade, *Le Chemin de Buenos Ayres* (The Road to Buenos Aires) by the French investigative journalist Albert Londres (1884-1932). Following the path of young French girls enticed from the port of Marseille to the Río de la Plata in the late 1920s, Londres managed to avoid any crude moralizing in what is essentially a journalistic description of the prostitutes' lives once they reached the Argentine capital. Like a true Parisian, he was disappointed at the regular grid-pattern streets, declaring that "walking about Buenos Aires is like playing draughts with one's feet. You feel like a piece being pushed from square to square on a draughts board." At the same time, he had a strong disdain for *porteño* showiness: "If the Argentines dared, they would walk around with an electric bulb up their backside."

But it was the dark side of life in the Argentine capital that interested Londres most. He headed for La Boca, in the 1920s the epicentre of prostitution, pornographic cinemas and opium dens. He joined a queue in one of the brothels, and was struck by how depressing both the male clients and the female whores were (the latter often having to "serve" as many as 75 men a day). He investigated further, to discover what happened to women who rebelled, became ill or grew old, and concluded that "we are all responsible" for this terrible blight.

By 1930 there was a growing campaign to control these seamy operations. Jewish organizations were particularly horrified that their own community should be running such a sordid business. Thanks to the former police chief Julio Alsogaray, the Zwi Migdal was denounced and closed down in 1930, and more than a hundred of its members given long prison sentences. However, the Jewish pimps appealed, and corrupt officials in the Justice Ministry released almost all of them. The injustice involved was so blatant that the public outcry forced the authorities to backtrack, and many of the Zwi Migdal members were sent back to prison—although nearly all of them escaped or were let out in the next few years, making their way to Uruguay or Brazil, where they began their activities all over again.

Similarly, the first attempts to criminalize prostitution failed because too many corrupt politicians and judges were clients or benefitted from generous kick-backs from the business. But in December 1935 Law 12,331 was passed, and as a result brothels were closed throughout the country (although in 1944 the incoming military government eased restrictions for garrison towns). Perón, the military officer who emerged as the great popular leader of Argentina in the late 1940s, reversed this decision in 1954. New legislation allowed "the installation of those establishments referred to by the Law of Social Prophylaxis". This was seen as an attack on the morality preached by the Catholic Church, and was another factor that led the various right-wing sectors in Argentine society and the military to join together and carry out a successful coup against him in 1955.

Moral Crusades

Another aspect of sexual activity that has often met with intolerance and repression in Buenos Aires is homosexuality. The first complaint about being singled out as a *manfrodita* or hermaphrodite came from an Englishman. In 1771, one William Higgings, director of the slave-importing South Sea Co. in Buenos Aires, filed a lawsuit against a silversmith for shouting this insult at him. By the 1880s there were already well-known meeting places for homosexuals in the city, in the so-called *barrios alegres* or gay neighbourhoods such as Plaza Mazzini or, once again, La Boca. At the turn of the century, several transvestites became famous for their criminal activities. One of the most widely known was Luis Fernández, nicknamed the "Bourbon Princess". His most audacious scheme was to claim he was a widow from the Paraguayan War (1864-70) and to petition Congress for a pension by faking the signature of President Roque Saenz Peña. Another was the Bella Otero, aka Culpino Alvarez. He/she would dress up as a woman and appear in wealthy homes to ask for donations to high-class charities. Culpino also found jobs as a maid, only to rob rich families after a few days in their employ. This larger-than-life individual further performed as a gypsy fortune teller with great success, and in 1903 published a book of homo-erotic poetry.

As with female prostitution, it was under the military governments from 1930 onwards that pressure, in particular from the Roman Catholic Church, began to increase on the capital's homosexuals. The most infamous of these scandals was the affair of more than thirty military cadets who were discovered and accused of being a "secret sect" determined to corrupt the youth of one of Argentina's "most prestigious institutions". This led to a widespread police roundup of the homosexual community. One of the cadets was sentenced to twelve years in jail; a well-known architect who was also convicted of taking part in these homosexual "orgies" committed suicide on his release. The scandal was one of the pre-texts for the 1943 military coup leaders insisting that they were on a "moral crusade" to clean up Argentina.

In 1944 a pseudo-scientific treatise appeared in a bestselling series entitled *Freud for Everyone*. In Volume Five on degenerate sex, Doctor J. Gómez Nerea attacked homosexuality in Argentina in the following terms:

> Here the problem is assuming frightening proportions. It is well-known that in the literary and artistic world of Buenos Aires there is a very high percentage of homosexuals. Actors, poets, prominent politicians, magistrates, all practise this terrible vice, and although society points its finger to stigmatise them, nothing can be done against them, because Argentine law has also suffered the influence of the libertine current that has Europe in its grip.

Gómez Nerea went on to claim that the Buenos Aires police had files on 20,000 homosexuals, and that their names should be published, so that "they can be avoided like lepers". A few pages on, the doctor went on to talk about Jews, whom he said had to be eliminated, and in true Nazi fashion included homosexuals into the bargain: "it is a defensive necessity for civilization, and will have to extend so far that one day the Jews, either through pogroms, mass executions, or modern practices of sterilization, will disappear from the planet. Just as homosexuality should disappear as well."

It is the Argentine sociologist Juan José Sebreli who has looked most closely at the persecution suffered by homosexuals in the Argentine capital, and noted how each military regime stepped up the campaign against them in the name of public morality. Sebreli further notes how the first Peronist governments from 1946 to 1954 played a double game in this respect: for several years, when Perón was seeking the backing of the Catholic Church, homosexuals were persecuted because they were seen as a threat to the family and procreation. But when the Catholic Church turned against Perón, at Christmas 1954, there was a massive roundup of homosexuals on the bizarre pretext that they had been corrupted by the religious mentality.

At the end of the 1950s and during the first half of the 1960s, there was a slight relaxation in attitudes. Sebreli remembers the port area, and in particular the Anchor Inn, a salon on the first floor of a café on the corner of Paseo Colón and San Juan. "Red light, mirrors, portraits of Queen Elizabeth and the Duke of Edinburgh, and a piano where the customers could play. The typical barmaid was here a legendary homosexual whose nickname was Cleopatra. This was the only place before the 1970s where men could dance together."

Once again the military takeover of power led to fresh problems. In the mid-1960s a campaign was launched against all public displays of sexual activity out-of-doors: heterosexual couples were arrested for kissing in public, and there were frequent police raids on the motels that were often the only places where unmarried couples could make love. There was also a crackdown on what were judged to be pornographic films, books and magazines. When General Onganía seized power in 1966, this campaign was intensified. According to Sebreli, "the few openly gay clubs were closed. Homosexual meeting places were destroyed; the toilets in some cinemas were cordoned off. Two spectacular operations were carried out: the first was in the Underground. One rush hour, the exits of all the stations were sealed simultaneously, and thousands of suspects who were loitering on the platforms and in the public toilets were arrested. The other roundup took place at the same time of day in the three classic cinemas for homosexual encounters on Calle Corrientes."

The Argentine writer Edgardo Cozarinsky has also written of the city centre cinemas that were famous in the 1950s for both homosexuals and female prostitution to ply their trade under cover of darkness. In his *Palacios plebeyos* (People's Palaces) describing the cinemas of Buenos Aires, he lists the celebrated "attractions" in the different city centre movie-houses, including the massive "Chino" from Rosario who in the Princesa "openly displayed his natural endowments to entice the unwary punter who might want to enjoy them. At the moment of contact, he would close his huge fist round the usually frail arm of the old man and demand he hand over his wallet, threatening to denounce him as 'amoral', 'degenerate' or for 'indecent acts in a public place'. These were journalistic rather than legal terms, but were more than enough to inspire terror in those years of institutionalised sexual repression."

The political violence of the 1970s made things still worse for any sexual alternatives. Even before the 1976 military coup, a right-wing Peronist magazine ran an article entitled "Getting Rid of Homosexuals" in which the author insisted that they should have "their hair cut or shaved in the street, and they should be left tied to trees with educational placards round their necks. We don't want any more homosexuals ... Marxism has used and continues to use homosexuals as a means of penetration [*sic*], and an ally of its objective."

This supposed link between subversive Marxism and subversive sexual behaviour was admirably portrayed in Manuel Puig's 1976 novel *Kiss of the Spider Woman,* in which Luis Molina, locked up for his "corruption of a minor", finds himself in the same cell as a political prisoner, Valentín. The book, with its frank discussion of homosexuality, could not be brought out in Argentina, but was one of the first Spanish-language published in Spain following the death of Franco.

During the latest military dictatorship from 1976 to 1983 there was yet another crackdown on homosexuals and lesbians, and the first openly gay organizations, Nuestro Mundo and Safo, were raided and closed down. Homosexuality was still considered as a disease, and as part of the "liberal moral decay" of western countries. In 1982, when General Galtieri tried to grab back the Malvinas/ Falklands Islands, Buenos Aires newspapers frequently carried articles about how degenerate the British forces were, lacking the true manliness of the Argentine male, and therefore little match for them militarily.

Since the return of democratic rule there has been marked progress in recognizing gay rights. The group Comunidad Homosexual Argentina was granted legal recognition early in the 1990s. The rights to benefits of same sex partners were also gradually recognized. Writers and playwrights openly discussed the topic in their works. A huge turning point came in July 2010 when same-sex marriages were legalized—although in typical Argentine fashion an appeal against this decision in Buenos Aires meant that the first male homosexual couple had to travel thousands of kilometres south to Tierra del Fuego to celebrate their wedding. In recent years, the Argentine capital has been promoted as a destination for gay tourists from abroad, although there is still a great deal of popular scorn for those who are seen as not true *machos*.

Military Terror

The fear on the streets of Buenos Aires in the 1970s and early 1980s came from the political chaos and then the stark repression initiated by the military dictatorship in March 1976. Prior to the military intervention bombs and shootouts were everyday dangers anywhere in the capital, and the number of kidnappings increased as the left-wing groups abducted businessmen for ransom, and right-wing groups also began kidnappings for political ends. Perhaps the most bizarre episode involved the kidnapping of the corpse of former military dictator General Aramburu. In 1970 the general had been abducted and then executed by the Montonero guerrillas as an act of "popular justice". Then in 1974 his body was stolen from the Recoleta cemetery, the traditional burial place of the "aristocracy" of Argentine society. The Montoneros said they would keep the corpse until the embalmed body of Eva Perón was brought back to Argentina for proper burial. For several weeks, the general's remains were ferried around Buenos Aires inside a petrol tanker until Evita—or the "illustrious mummy"—was brought back from Spain and buried in the Duarte family vault in the same Recoleta cemetery (where it is still one of the main attractions for visitors from Argentina and elsewhere).

After 1976 the fear felt by ordinary citizens in the Argentine capital was palpable. During the day army trucks would race down the streets, seal off a block or a building and soldiers would rush inside. Passersby, passengers on buses or car drivers learned to look the other way, not to comment on anything, not to ask any questions. The saddest and most frequently heard comment was *por algo será*, "there must be some reason for it". Police stations throughout the capital were surrounded by walls of sandbags, with police and army personnel barricaded behind them weapons at the ready. At night the fear became even greater. Cinemas, theatres, cafés and restaurants were often deserted, as it was enough to be caught by the security forces without an identity document to be hauled off and never seen again. And after midnight the *grupos de tarea* or task forces began their work. In groups of eight, ten or more—often mostly youngsters doing their military service or *colimba*, led by an officer or two—these were the agents who "disappeared" people. They took them off to secret detention centres, where they would be tortured to give the names of their colleagues or planned guerrilla actions, then killed, often in the most violent way. The security forces never admitted they had snatched anyone and families had no-one they could turn to: the police were working with the military; the judiciary was either cowed or in favour of what was going on; politicians had been thrown out of Congress, and were often imprisoned themselves; the churches, and in particular the hierarchy of the Roman Catholic faith, were frequently supporters of the dictatorship, as they regarded the left-wing guerrillas as godless and evil; foreign embassies could do little for citizens from their countries. In the years between 1976 and 1983 Argentina suffered its own version of the "final solution": in order to rid society of what the military leaders liked to call the "cancer of subversion" they decided not to arrest and try people (most of them youths) for alleged offences, but simply to eliminate them. Hundreds of their victims were buried in mass graves in the suburbs of Buenos Aires; many more were taken up in planes and thrown out (some apparently still alive) into the brown, muddy waters of the Río de la Plata.

Thankfully, this darkest period in the recent history of the Argentine capital came to an end in 1984 with the return of civilian rule, although the scars from those days are still visible. The worst of the secret detention centres, the Navy School of Mechanics near Avenida del Libertador in Nuñez, where human rights groups claim some 5,000 people were tortured, was at first turned into a military academy. The city authorities protested that this was a blatant attempt to pretend that the dreadful events that had taken place there had never happened, with the result that in 2004 the site was turned over to the government of Buenos Aires. It now functions as a Space for Memory and the Promotion of Human Rights. Other torture centres, such as the Club Atlético, located close to the spot where Juan de Garay landed in 1580, are just blank walls.

Under President Raúl Alfonsín, citizens were encouraged to go and present denunciations of suspected human rights crimes—but to their local police stations, when more often than not the people there had either participated in or turned a blind eye to the horrors of the dictatorship. Sometimes those who were dismissed from the police or other security forces continued with violent activities, abducting people and committing robberies without any political excuse: the rates of violent crime in Buenos Aires increased dramatically. Fortunately, although there were short-lived military uprisings against President Alfonsín, since 1984 Buenos Aires has not been the scene of violent domestic political battles. Yet in the 1990s, under President Carlos Menem, conflicts from which Argentina is normally shielded by geographical distance and lack of direct involvement twice brought violent death to its streets. In 1992 suicide bombers smashed a pick-up truck into the Israeli Embassy on Suipacha and Arroyo in the centre of the city. The building was almost completely destroyed, and 29 people were killed, including several elderly residents in the home run by Franciscan nuns on the opposite side of the street.

Two year later, in July1994, another car bomb struck the AMIA, the Jewish Mutual Aid Association. More than eighty people died in the blast and several hundred were wounded on the crowded streets of the traditional Jewish garment area of Once. No-one was ever brought to justice for either attack, although Jewish groups and journalists have argued that they were carried out by a Hezbollah group, under instructions from Iran. More disturbingly, it was widely alleged that the Menem government had accepted massive bribes in order to let the terrorists who committed these atrocities in and out of Argentina. Yet again, nothing has ever been proved.

Strangely perhaps, in recent years the most troubled parts of the city are once more the *orillas*, those areas where the federal capital meets the province of Buenos Aires. The inhabitants of wealthy suburbs to the north and west of the city find they are living alongside shantytown dwellers who exist on next-to-nothing. As was the case more than 150 years ago, it is the new migrants who are regarded with the most suspicion. In the nineteenth century it was the influx of Spaniards and Italians that was seen as a threat to decent, "civilized" life in the Argentine capital. Nowadays it is the Bolivians and Paraguayans, thousands of whom leave their own poorer countries in search of work, who are regarded as dirty, disruptive and criminal.

THE DARK SIDE

Mar del Plata: mass tourism (Leandro Kibisz/Wikimedia Commons)

12 | Surroundings
The City's Hinterland

Today's flights from Europe or the United States give only a faint sense of just how distant Buenos Aires must have seemed to the early explorers and settlers. Even so, after hours high above the blue of the Atlantic and then the vast green expanse of Brazil, it still comes as a shock to gaze down first on the muddy brown waters of the Río de la Plata, then the pale green of the flatlands of the pampas and, all of a sudden, the concrete, mushroom-like skyscrapers of the city. From 30,000 feet, the Argentine capital appears not only as a surprise, but as a mistake, set down so far from anywhere else. Indeed, in a short story called *The Mistake*, the contemporary Argentine author Martín Kohan has written:

> Buenos Aires exists on the edge of a mistake. It was even founded on the edge of that mistake. Because the first navigators to reach this river, their eyes on the lookout for the new, thought they had come across a sea. They thought that because it was so huge, despite the lack of salt in the water. They called it the Mar Dulce, the Sweet Sea, and yet they were wrong. Eventually they accepted it was a river, even though it was incredibly wide, and called it the Río de la Plata, or River Plate, hoping it would lead to riches. Which it didn't, meaning they were doubly mistaken. They were also mistaken when they sailed up it, calculating that in addition to its riches of silver, the river would bring them geographical riches too: the sea passage between two oceans, the shortcut for commerce that was finally discovered some years later by exploring the ends of the earth, or many years later by chopping Panama in two.

In a similar vein, the Argentine Foreign Minister under President Carlos Menem in the 1990s used to insist that because of its history as an immigrant nation Argentina was a European country that by accident found itself several thousand kilometres from its neighbours. As a result, he instructed the Argentine delegation at the United Nations to vote with "fellow" Europeans rather than following the positions adopted by the other countries of Latin America (except of course when it came to voting on the question of the sovereignty of the Malvinas/Falklands Islands).

While for centuries the land border to the south and west of Buenos Aires came under threat from raids by the indigenous tribes of the pampas, the Río de la Plata itself was also the scene of many battles over the years. In colonial times, Argentina had to fight against the Portuguese in Brazil for control of its waters, as well as beating off excursions from the Dutch, French and British, who were all anxious to gain the upper hand and dominate trade in the estuary. It was the British who were also involved in the last great naval battle to take place here. This was during the Second World War, when three British cruisers tracked down the formidable *Admiral Graf Spee* in December 1939 to the mouth of the river. Badly damaged after several days of combat, the German heavy cruiser sought refuge in the neutral port of Montevideo, before eventually emerging and being scuttled in order to avoid capture. This "Battle of the River Plate" was hailed in Britain as a much-needed triumph early in the war. The German captain and as many as a thousand of the *Admiral Graf Spee*'s crew crossed to Buenos Aires, where the captain shot himself. Some of the German survivors stayed on in Argentina, joining German communities already established in Córdoba, Santa Fe or the province of Buenos Aires.

Islands and Deltas

Before they dispersed in Argentina, many of the German crew were held on Martín García, the largest island at the mouth of the River north-west of the capital, and named after one of the sailors who were buried there during Juan de Solís' 1580 expedition downriver to found Buenos Aires. In the centuries that followed, the island was fought over by the different powers that sought to control shipping in the estuary. In 1845, for example, it was captured by Giuseppe Garibaldi, who at that time was fighting for the

Uruguayans against the Argentines. In the twentieth century Martín García often functioned as a prison for deposed presidents Hipólito Yrigoyen spent a year here after the first military coup in 1930. General Perón spent some days on the island in 1955 before seeking refuge in Paraguay, while in the 1960s it was the turn of the unfortunate Arturo Frondizi. In more recent times, Martín García, which has a small resident population of less than two hundred, has become a nature reserve and a tourist destination for trippers from the Tigre Delta.

"El Tigre", said to have been named after the River Tigris in Mesopotamia, is an area of almost 13,000 square kilometres to the north of Buenos Aires where the River Paraná splits into many smaller tributaries which pour into the Río de la Plata estuary. The silt they bring down from the heart of the South American continent has formed more than 3,000 small islands, many of which have been used since the middle of the nineteenth century as places for retreat and recreation outside the grime and noise of the capital. President Domingo Sarmiento helped make the delta islands a fashionable place in the 1860s, especially after 1865, when the first railway line was built, reducing the journey time for the thirty or so kilometres from the capital from a day to only a hour. Nowadays there is a tourist train, *el tren de la costa*, which makes the same journey in more or less the same length of time, passing such delights as the Tierra Santa along the way. Billed in Argentina as the "first religious theme park in the world", this is a tacky recreation of the Holy Land, complete with actors playing everyone from Jesus Christ to the shepherds with their flocks. Or there is the epic bus journey in the cream coloured *colectivo* no. 60, which travels day and night from Constitución in the heart of the city to the market place in the town of Tigre.

The 1871 yellow fever epidemic in the capital also led to the upper classes building houses here as a refuge. It was the British in particular who flocked to the Tigre Delta, where they founded the Tigre Boat Club in 1888, and created mansions that are still seen as typically British. Other European immigrant communities followed suit, with the Italians and Germans also establishing rowing clubs on the riverfront in the town of Tigre. Many of the islands contain only one property, which can vary from the ultra-luxurious to simple shacks with corrugated iron roofs. Isobel Strachey in her 1947 novel *A Summer in Buenos Aires* evokes the atmosphere of peace and calm that so attracts residents of the capital: "boat-houses made of light planks or corrugated iron painted white and deep blue sloped into the brown lapping water, alternating with long banks of hydrangea bushes with great, round, light blue flowers and light green leaves; behind these were little white chalets and bungalows covered with trellis-work and long wooden balconies and verandas."

There are no roads in the delta itself, and so everything has to be ferried by boat. In the more accessible spots there are sports clubs for the trade unions, while hidden away on more remote islands are exclusive gated communities. After many years of neglect, with polluted, smelly waters and rundown facilities, the Tigre Delta has been redeveloped in recent times and has attracted back not only tourists but some of the wealthier inhabitants of Buenos Aires.

The River Paraná is still an important trade route. Rosario and Santa Fe have traditionally been its main ports for grain exports from the pampas. The river is also the link with the subtropical north of Argentina: the area between here and the River Uruguay is often known as Mesopotamia. Further north are two of Argentina's main tourist attractions: the Iguazú falls and the remains of the eighteenth-century Jesuit settlements for Guaraní Indians. This is where Argentina truly links with the rest of South America, where the atmosphere and way of life have little to do with the frantic rhythm of the capital. Rosario's most famous son was one of those who made the journey down from the subtropical north of Misiones—although he was largely unaware of it, still being in-side his mother's womb. This was Ernesto "Che" Guevara, the son of Ernesto Guevara Lynch. Guevara Lynch often tried out busi-ness schemes that came to nothing. Attracted by the boom in *yerba mate* tea plantations, he bought land in Misiones some nineteen hundred kilometres north of Buenos Aires and in 1927 his whole family there. When his wife Celia became pregnant with the young Ernesto, they thought it prudent to make the long river journey down to the more advanced city of Rosario, where she gave birth to the future revolutionary on 14 May 1928. They did not stay long in the city, however, presenting the new-born baby shortly afterwards to their relatives in Buenos Aires. Not long after that, with the *mate* plantation turning out to be yet another of Guevara Lynch's failures, and Che's asthmatic tendencies being made worse by the heat and humidity in the north, the family left the region for good. Perhaps it was these first two trips through the heart of South America that gave the young Ernesto a taste for exploring and experiencing the life of his continent.

Across the Estuary

Another of the projects Che Guevara's father was involved in during the 1920s was a boatyard in the north of Buenos Aires. The Guevaras' social life, like that of the most prosperous *porteños*, revolved around the San Isidro Yacht Club. From there sailing aficionados can race or drift slowly around the estuary, or cross it to Uruguay. Almost directly across from Buenos Aires is the colonial town of Colonia del Sacramento. This is the oldest town in Uruguay, first founded on its peninsula by the Portuguese in the seventeenth century. Over the following two centuries, Colonia was fought over many times, changing hands between Argentina and Brazil until in 1828 it became part of what is known as the República de la Banda Oriental (the eastern bank of the Río de la Plata, or Uruguay). Nowadays its historic fortified centre and churches are a UNESCO World Heritage site, and the thousands of Argentines who flock here at weekends and in the summer months (fast hydrofoils make the crossing in less than an hour) are more intent on having a good time than on fighting.

Colonia's beaches are as muddy as those across the Río de la Plata, and so for sand and sun the Argentines head further east towards the Atlantic on the Uruguayan bank of the estuary. There are some resorts around the capital, Montevideo, which is eighty kilometres across the Río de la Plata from Buenos Aires. First settled, like the Argentine capital, because it was on a promontory and therefore offering a strong defensive position (its name is said to come from a sailor crying out "Monte-video"—"I see a mountain") it is nowadays a city of close to one and a half million people. As such, it is regarded by many *porteños* as much smaller and slower than their own metropolis, but it does have a distinct identity of its own. However, most vacationing Argentines head to the tip of the estuary, where the Uruguayan coast turns north into the waters of the Atlantic. Here the best-known resort is Punta del Este, whose population swells from less than 10,000 in the winter to over half a million in the summer months from Christmas to the end of March. Thousands of *porteños* make the short flight across here for two or three weeks of holiday each summer: the warmer, shallow waters are ideal for young children.

Punta del Este itself has become so overcrowded that in recent years it has become more chic to rent or even buy on the other side of the peninsula, where the Atlantic provides stronger waves, and until recently the accommodation was much more basic. With a population of only a little over three million, Uruguay's economy depends to a large extent on foreign tourists, and its beaches area barometer of which of its neighbours are doing best economically: in the years of crisis in Argentina in 2001 and 2002 far fewer came to Uruguay, but their places were taken by Chileans and Brazilians. Now all the Southern Cone countries are enjoying a period of economic stability and growth, and the beaches of Punta del Este are thronged again.

To the Pampas

To the west and south of Buenos Aires, the city's suburbs soon merge into the vast pampa heartlands. At the weekends and on longer holidays, tens of thousands of *porteños* clog the Panamerican Highway to get out of the city and into the countryside. The better-off may belong to a *country*, usually a gated club where they can meet up with their neighbours from the capital, share an *asado*, play tennis or paddle while their children swim or play in the open air. The less wealthy head for the clubs organized by their trade unions or by the Peronist political party; as president, Perón was the first to introduce paid holidays, and encouraged social activities for the workers. Often the city dwellers, as well as tourists out for the day or weekend from Buenos Aires, visit some of the "typical" towns where life is still built around agriculture. Such places include the historic town of San Antonio de Areco, which has become a favourite destination for tourists from Buenos Aires, while nearby is the *estancia* and the small museum commemorating the novel *Don Segundo Sombra*, after *Martín Fierro* the most important book about *gaucho* life, written here by the landowner Ricardo Guiraldes in the 1920s. Don Segundo, based on a real-life *gaucho*, represents all the mythical values of the indomitable Argentine cowboy: fiercely independent, intensely loyal, at one with the natural world around him. Nowadays the *gauchos* are more likely to put on a show for the tourists, wrestling young bullocks to the ground, performing tricks on horseback or dancing the *malambo* or other country dances dressed in their ponchos and black *bombachas* or baggy trousers, with their *facones* or long knives stuck in their belt.

Beyond these tourist towns, with their carefully restored *pulperías* or general stores, their *tambos* or dairies selling local cheeses and tubs of *dulce de leche* and the *talabarterías* with leather and woven goods produced on the pampas—often following original indigenous patterns—the working *estancias* continue with their cattle-rearing and wheat growing much as they have done for two centuries. The small towns dotting the pampas often look very similar. They probably grew up round a railway halt in the latter years of the nineteenth century. Often a particular immigrant community settled there—Italian, Spanish, Swiss or *sirio-libanés*, giving the town its own particular flavour. But they are all chequerboard developments, usually of one-storey houses round a central square where the church, the local municipal government and the main store/bar are situated. The middle of the square is usually a garden, with trees whitewashed against harmful insects, and in the centre the bust or a grander equestrian state of General San Martín or some other national hero. This part of the pampas close to Buenos Aires continues with traditional agriculture, although increasingly vast tracts of fertile land are now being turned over to producing soya, which brings quicker profits to the farmer. Much of this soya is genetically modified, and so has aroused controversy with ecological groups, although the government seems to have no qualms about its implications.

About sixty kilometres north-west of the city of Buenos Aires is the most important Christian site in Argentina. The Basilica de Nuestra Señora de Luján is at the heart of the town of the same name. In a chapel behind the main altar stands the tiny statue of the Virgin of Luján, the patron saint of Argentina. Legend has it that as long ago as 1630 the statue was being carted from Brazil to Buenos Aires, but that all attempts to get the wagon beyond Luján failed, so that it was taken off the cart and a shrine built to the Virgin on this spot. Millions of Catholic Argentines visit the basilica each year, many of them coming on foot from the capital to keep promises they have made to the Virgin. The basilica itself is a large neo-gothic disappointment, finally completed in 1937 after almost fifty years.

When the Argentine economy is shaky, many more inhabitants of the capital return again to resorts on their own Atlantic coastline. The most traditional and by far the largest of these is Mar del Plata, some four hundred kilometres south-east of Buenos Aires. Every January and February, hundreds of thousands of the city dwellers uproot themselves and head for its sandy beaches—often to swim, drink *mate*, play football and eat *asados* with the same people they have been mixing with all the other months of the year back in the capital. Mar del Plata first became famous in the 1930s for its casino (then reputed to be the largest in the world) as well as the calm, shallow waters that lap its many beaches. In the 1940s and 1950s it was by far the most popular resort in Argentina; proud Argentines would come back from their forays to the Mediterranean or the Caribbean only to proudly assert: *como Mar del Plata no hay* ("there's nowhere like Mar del Plata"). Since those days, younger people have chosen instead to go to smaller, livelier resorts further up the coast such as Pinamar or Villa Gesell. The contemporary Argentine author Alan Pauls spent fifteen summers in the latter resort in his childhood, and in *La vida descalzo* (The Barefoot Life) describes his memories of those holidays: "Villa Gesell is the historical (and personal) proof of the Platonic idea of the beach as a neutral, absorbent surface, the blank screen *par excellence*, and thus (which explains the threat of ruin always hanging over it) it is the *non plus ultra* of the conquistador, the explorer, the pioneer, who can afford the luxury of projecting onto it the most arbitrary images without feeling guilty that he is going against original nature of any kind."

Between the coastal resorts and the capital, the only city of any importance is the provincial capital, La Plata. Although it is less than 65 kilometres from Buenos Aires, life here is much more relaxed and slow. Created in 1880 when Buenos Aires became the federal capital of the republic, it was built according to one of the first comprehensive city plans, with chequerboard streets, diagonal avenues and parks every six blocks. It also boasts a famous zoo and several important museums, above all the Museo de Ciencias Naturales (Museum of Natural Sciences). Together with this, the city's university has traditionally attracted students from all over Latin America to study natural or veterinary sciences. In 1945 Juan Domingo Perón married Eva Duarte in La Plata, and after her death in 1952 the city was renamed Ciudad Evita, but its original name was reinstated after Perón was toppled from power in 1955.

It is a journey of several hundred kilometres to the west or north-west of Buenos Aires before there are any other major cities. The route to the north-west leads to Argentina's second city of Córdoba. This was founded in 1573, before the capital, and contains many more reminders of the country's colonial past. For two centuries, this was the route for all trade with Spain—up through Córdoba, Tucumán, Salta and then Bolivia, and many of the riches brought by trade can still be seen in the form of extravagant churches and other buildings. The province of Córdoba also boasts the first mountains or *sierras* to be found beyond the levels of the pampas, and this has made it another popular holiday destination for many who wish to get away from the overheated and overcrowded capital. To the west, it is more than 950 kilometres before there is another city of any great size. Mendoza in fact nestles in the foothills of the Andes mountains, which form Argentina's western border all the way down from north to south. The centre of the country's wine industry, Mendoza is a prosperous, bustling place that also serves as the link to neighbouring Chile.

The emptiness around the capital only serves to reinforce the feeling of an enclosed, self-contained space. The city clings to the edge of the land, and goes about its own business largely ignoring not only the reat of Argentina, but the American continent as a whole. And though it has grown up over the centuries next to the 'unmoving' Rio de la Plata, the writer Julio Cortázar paradoxically compares the city itself to a wave, constantly moving and changing:

Inmovil en sus cimientos,
Buenos Aires es una ola que se repite
Al infinito,
Siempre la misma para el indiferente
Y cada vez otra
Para el que mira su cresta,
La curva de su lomo,
La manera de alzarse y de romper.

Unmoving on its foundations,
Buenos Aires is a wave repeated
To infinity,
Always the same to the uninterested
And forever different
For whoever looks at its crest,
The curve of its back,
The way it has of rising and breaking.

Further Reading

Abós, Alvaro (ed.), *El libro de Buenos Aires: Crónicas de cinco siglos*. Buenos Aires: Grijalbo, 2000.

Archetti, Eduardo P., *Masculinities: Football, Polo and the Tango in Argentina*. Oxford: Berg, 1999.

Arlt, Roberto, *Aguasfuertes porteñas*. Buenos Aires, Losada 1994.

Benítez, Carlos Pedro José, *Buenos Aires, Síntesis histórica y poblacional*. Buenos Aires: Editorial Epsilon, 1983.

Bergero, Adriana J., *Intersecting Tango: Cultural Geographies of Buenos Aires, 1900-1930*. Pittsburgh: University of Pittsburgh Press, 2008.

Bioy Casares, Adolfo, *Memoria sobre la pampa y los gauchos*. Buenos Aires: Sur, 1970.

Caimari, Lila, *Apenas un delincuente: Crimen, Castigo y Cultura en la Argentina, 1880-1955*. Buenos Aires: Siglo XXI, 2004.

Caistor, Nick, *In Focus: Argentina*. London: Latin America Bureau, 1996.

Collier, Simon, *The Life, Music, and Times of Carlos Gardel*. Pittsburgh: University of Pittsburgh Press, 1986.

Cozarinsky, Edgardo, *Palacios plebeyos*. Buenos Aires: Editorial Sudamericana, 2006.

Crawley, Eduardo, *A House Divided, Argentina 1880-1980*. New York: St Martin's Press, 1984.

Darwin, Charles, *The Voyage of the Beagle*. London: Wordsworth Classics of World Literature, 1997.

Di Giovanni, Norman Thomas, *The Lesson of the Master: On Borges and his Work*. London: Continuum, 2004.

Di Tella, Torcuato, *Historia social de la Argentina contemporánea*. Buenos Aires: Editorial Troquel, 1998.

Durrell, Gerald, *The Drunken Forest*. London: Hart-Davis, 1956.

Ferrer, Aldo, *Living Within Our Means*. Boulder CO: Westview, 1985.

Foster, David William, *Buenos Aires, the City and Cultural Production*. Gainesville FL: University of Florida Press, 1998.

France, Miranda, *Bad Times in Buenos Aires*. London: Weidenfeld & Nicolson, 1998.

Graham-Yooll, Andrew, *A State of Fear*. London: Eland, 1986.

Graham-Yooll, Andrew, *The Forgotten Colony. A History of the English-speaking Communities in Argentina*. London: Hutchinson, 1981.

Guy, Donna J, *Sex and Danger in Buenos Aires*. Lincoln NE: University of Nebraska Press, 1991.

Hudson, W. H., *Far Away and Long Ago*. London: Eland, 2001.

Kaminsky, Amy, *Argentina: Stories for a Nation*. Minneapolis: University of Minnesota Press, 2008.

Kassabova, Kapka, *Twelve Minutes of Love: A Tango Story*. London: Portobello, 2011.

Keeling, David J., *Buenos Aires: Global Dreams, Local Crisis*. Chichester: Wiley, 1996.

Makarius, Sameer, *Buenos Aires, mi ciudad*. Buenos Aires: Editorial Universitaria de Buenos Aires, 1963.

Martínez Estrada, Ezequiel, *La cabeza de Goliat*. Madrid: Editorial Revista de Occidente, 1970.

Mason, T., *Passion of the People? Football in South America*. London: Verso, 1995.

Matamoro, Blas, *Historia del tango*. Buenos Aires: Centro Editor de América Latina, 1971.

Naipaul, V. S., *The Return of Eva Perón*. London: Heinemann, 1980.

Neuman, Andrés, *Una vez Argentina*. Barcelona: Editorial Anagrama, 2003.

Nunca Más: Report on the Disappearance of Persons. London: Faber & Faber with Index on Censorship, 1986.

Pauls, Alan, *La vida descalza*. Buenos Aires: Editorial Sudamericana, 2006.

Pauls, Alan, *The Past*. Translated by Nick Caistor. London: Vintage Books, 2008.

Pujol, Sergio, *Discépolo*. Buenos Aires: Emecé Editores, 1996.

Randall, Laura, *An Economic History of Argentina in the Twentieth Century*. New York: Columbia University Press, 1978.

Redfern, Walter, *Writing on the Move: Albert Londres and Investigative Journalism*. Bern: Peter Lang, 2004.

Reid, Michael, *Forgotten Continent: the Battle for Latin America's Soul*. New Haven: Yale University Press, 2007.

Romero, José Luis, *Breve historia de la Argentina*. Buenos Aires: Editorial Universitaria de Buenos Aires, 1965.

Ross, Stanley R. and Thomas F. McGann (eds.), *Buenos Aires, 400 Years*. Austin: University of Texas Press, 1982.

Salas, Horacio, *El Tango*. Buenos Aires: Editorial Planeta, 1986.

Schávelzon, Daniel, *The Historical Archaeology of Buenos Aires*. New York: Kluwer Academic/Plenum Publishers, 1999.

Scobie, James R., *Buenos Aires, Plaza to Suburb, 1870-1910*. New York: Oxford University Press, 1974.

Schoo, Ernesto, *Mi Buenos Aires querido*. Valencia, Spain: Pre-Textos, 2011.

Sebreli, Juan José, *Escritos sobre escritos, ciudades bajo ciudades*. Buenos Aires: Editorial Sudamericana, 1997.

Soriano, Osvaldo, *Rebeldes, soñadores y fugitivos*. Buenos Aires: Editora 12, 1987.

Ulla, Noemí, *Tango, rebelión y nostalgia*. Buenos Aires: Centro Editor de América Latina, 1982.

Vázquez-Rial, Horacio, *Buenos Aires 1880-1930, La capital de un imperio imaginario*. Madrid: Alianza Editorial, 1996.

Wilson, Jason, *Borges, A Critical Life*. London: Reaktion, 2006.

Wilson, Jason, *Buenos Aires: a Cultural and Literary Companion*. Oxford: Signal, 1999.

Fiction and Poetry

Arlt, Roberto, *The Seven Madmen*. (trans. Nick Caistor). London: Serpent's Tail, 1984.

Borges, Jorge Luis, *Collected Fictions*. (trans. Andrew Hurley). London: Viking Penguin, 1998.

Borges, Jorge Luis, *Selected Poems*. London: Penguin, 2000.

Costantini, Humberto, *The Long Night of Francisco Sanctis*. (trans. Norman Thomas di Giovanni). London: Picador, 1984.

Cozarinsky, Edgardo, *The Moldavian Pimp*. (trans. Nick Caistor). London: Harvill Secker, 2007.

Cozarinsky, Edgardo, *Urban Voodoo*. New York: Lumen Books, 1990.

Echeverria, Esteban, *The Slaughteryard*. (trans. Norman Thomas di Giovanni). London: Harper Collins, 2010.

Eloy Martínez, Tomás, *Santa Evita*. London: Transworld, 1997.

Eloy Martínez, Tomás, *The Perón Novel*. New York: Knopf, 1999.

Eloy Martínez, Tomás, *The Tango Singer*. London: Bloomsbury, 2006.

Kohan, Martín, *Seconds Out*. London: Serpent's Tail, 2010.

Kohan, Martín, *School for Patriots*. London: Serpent's Tail, 2012.

Marechal, Leopoldo, *Adán Buenosayres*. Buenos Aires: Editorial Sudamericana, 1999.

Sábato, Ernesto, *Sobre héroes y tumbas*. Buenos Aires: Fabril Editores, 1961.

Vázquez Montalban, Manuel, *The Buenos Aires Quintet*. London: Serpent's Tail, 2003.

Index